EAT BEAUTIFUL
grain-free, sugar-free and loving it

A COOKBOOK BY
MEGAN STEVENS

To receive free bonus videos with additional grain-free, sugar-free recipes and an explanation of the new grain-free baking technique utilized in this book, sign up here:
www.eatbeautiful.net/free-videos

TABLE OF CONTENTS

CHAPTER ONE: *Waffles, Pancakes and Crepes*

Waffle #1—"Carrot Cake" | 12
   Carrot Flour | 14
Waffle #2—"Yellow Cake" | 15
   Granny Smith Applesauce | 16
Waffle #3—Sprouted Nut | 17
Waffle #4—Chocolate Chia Seed | 19
Macadamia Nut Pancakes with Coconut Syrup | 22
   Coconut Syrup | 24
AIP Pancakes | 25
Crepes | 27
   Homemade Hemp or Nut Milk | 29

CHAPTER TWO: *Scones and Scuffins*

Traditional Scones | 33
Almond-Blueberry Scones | 35
Cashew-Blueberry Scuffins | 37

CHAPTER THREE: *Loaves and Muffins*

Zucchini Bread | 42
Blueberry Tea Bread | 44
Chocolate Berry Soufflé Muffins | 46
Savory Meat and Veggie Muffins, a k a Sausage and Egg Muffins | 48
Sloppy Joe Muffins | 50
Traditional Versatile Muffins | 52
Chocolate-Fig-Walnut Muffins | 55

Apple Cinnamon Breakfast Muffins | 57
    Chocolate-Peanut Butter-Banana Muffin Variation | 58
    Pumpkin-Chocolate Chip Muffin Variation | 58

CHAPTER FOUR: *Bars and Cookies*

Traditional Chocolate Chip Cookies | 60
Vegan, Egg-free Chocolate Chip Cookies | 63
Nut-free Chocolate Chip Cookies | 65
Bacon-Chocolate Chip-Walnut Cookies | 67
Halvah Cookies | 69
Breakfast Porridge Apple Cookies | 71
Classic Pumpkin Spice Cookies | 73
"Oatmeal-Raisin" Cookies | 75
Macadamia Nut Snickerdoodles | 77
Chocolate Chip Cake Bars | 79
    Pumpkin Chocolate Chip Cake Bar Variation | 80
Pumpkin Pie Bars with Chocolate-Lined Crust | 81
Pumpkin Cream Cheese Bars | 85
Gooey Brownies | 88

CHAPTER FIVE: *Pies*

Kiwi Lime Pie | 92
    Happy Omega Pie Crust | 92
Mixed Berry-Avocado Pie | 94
    Brazil Nut Crust | 95
Carrot-Cinnamon Mousse Pie | 97
    Italian Nut or Seed Pie Crust | 97
Pumpkin Pie | 99
    Simple Nut Crust | 99
Traditional Baked Pumpkin Pie | 102
    Sweet Nut Crust | 102
Chocolate Maple Pecan Pie | 104
    Cashew Pastry Crust | 104
Blackberry (or Apple) Pie | 106
    Date Nut Crust | 106

Chocolate Cream Pie | 109
Lemon Meringue Pie | 111
Raw Strawberry-Lemon Cream Pie | 114
   Raw Crust | 114

CHAPTER SIX: *Cakes and Frostings*

Chocolate Cake with Chocolate Frosting | 118
   Chocolate Ganache Frosting | 119
   Chocolate Frosting (xylitol-sweetened) | 120
Chocolate Cupcakes | 121
Chocolate Beet Cake | 123
Chocolate-Avocado-Date-Pudding Frosting | 124
Carrot Cake | 125
   Classic Cream Cheese Frosting with Honey | 127
   "Cream Cheese" Frosting (dairy-free) | 128
Zucchini Spice Chocolate Cake | 129
Apple Cake (xylitol-sweetened) | 131
   Hazelnut "Buttercream" Frosting (dairy-free) | 133
   Cashew "Buttercream" (xylitol-sweetened) | 133
   Cashew "Buttercream" (dairy-free, stevia-sweetened) | 134

CHAPTER SEVEN: *Easy Eggs, Clafouti and Porridges*

Berry Clafouti | 138
Steamed Eggs | 141
Marshmallow Root and Slippery Elm Porridge for One | 143
Sweet Collard Greens Porridge with Blueberries | 145
Winter Squash Porridge | 147

CHAPTER EIGHT: *Savory Breads, Pizza, Rolls and Casseroles*

Sweet Sandwich Rolls, or Bittersweet Chocolate Sandwich Rolls | 152
Loaf Bread, for Sandwiches or Not | 154
Panini | 156
Yorkshire Pudding "Polenta" Cake | 159
Pizza Dough | 161
Herbed Dairy-free Ricotta | 163
Beef Stew En Croute | 164

Slow-cooked Pork Cobbler | 167

Shepherd's Pie | 170

CHAPTER NINE: *Toppings, Sauces, Custards, Puddings and Compotes*

Chocolate Crème Fraiche | 176

Chocolate Sauce | 178

Vanilla Bean Crème Fraiche | 179

Russian Crème Fraiche | 180

Fully Cultured Raw Yogurt | 182

Coconut Whipped Cream | 184

Vanilla Custard (dairy-free) | 186

Hemp Scoopable Custard with Whole Raspberries | 188

    Hemp Milk | 189

Traditional Blintz Filling | 191

Dairy-Free Blintz Filling | 192

Vanilla Date Shake "Ice Cream" | 193

Dark Chocolate "Ice Cream" | 194

The Best Frozen Yogurt | 195

Carrot Cinnamon Frozen Yogurt | 197

Straight-up Ice Cream | 198

Cranberry-Mixed Berry Compote | 199

Raw Jam | 201

Chocolate-Avocado Pudding, Frosting or Fudge | 202

Blender Chocolate Mousse (dairy-free) | 204

Marionberry "Yogurt" | 206

Strawberry-Walnut Pate | 207

Pumpkin Butter with Strawberries | 208

Peanut Butter Sauce | 210

CHAPTER TEN: *Beverages*

Homemade Coconut Milk | 214

Creamy Warm Horchata Eggnog | 215

Hot Chocolate (dairy-free) | 217

Beet Kvass with Raspberries | 218

Stevia Lemonade | 220

Tarragon or Basil Limeade with Honey | 221

"Juiced Tea" — Marionberry Rooibos with Honey | 222
Honey-Spice Lassi | 223
Cardamom-Rose Water Lassi | 224
Cilantro-Mint Lassi (dairy-free) | 225
Chia Electrolyte Beverage | 226
Ginger-Honey Milkshake | 227

CHAPTER ELEVEN: *Feeding Kids*

Marionberry Panna Cotta (dairy-free) | 232
Cultured Gelatin Americana | 234
Colorful Gelatin | 235
    Cucumber-Tarragon/Mint | 235
    Strawberry-Lime | 236
    Blueberry-Beet | 236
    Vanilla-Rooibos | 236
    Green Tea-Spirulina | 236
Pumpkin Spice Pudding (dairy-free) | 238
Rooibos Chia Chai Horchata (dairy-free) | 240
Chia Seed Porridge with Apples (dairy-free) | 241
Chocolate-Cinnamon Chia Porridge, or "Aztec Chia Porridge" (dairy-free) | 242
Easy Almond Butter Ice Cream (dairy-free) | 244
Crème Fraiche Parfaits | 245
Clafouti Parfaits | 247
Dairy-Free Parfaits | 247
Egg-Free and/or Dairy-Free Parfaits | 248

CHAPTER TWELVE: *Foods NOT to Eat (and Why)* | 249

CHAPTER THIRTEEN: *Glossary of Ingredients* | 255

APPENDIX 1: *Recommended Sources for Food and Equipment* | 267

APPENDIX 2: *Methods* | 270

APPENDIX 3: *AIP Recipes* | 273

FOREWORD

"Kindred spirits are not so scarce as I used to think. It's splendid to find out there are so many of them in the world." —L.M. MONTGOMERY, IN ANNE OF GREEN GABLES

I met Megan at a small group Bible study when we were both in college in Salem, Oregon. The chairs were arranged in a circle, for intimacy, and she was sitting directly across from me. When she spoke, I knew we were kindred spirits. I felt just like I imagine Anne Shirley did when she first met Diana Barry.

What was it that drew me to Megan? She was so obviously filled with joy, hope and love. It was palpable in every word and every smile. I thought to myself then and there that I hoped we would be friends. Dreams do come true, because we soon became *dear* friends.

And as dear friends tend to do, we connected over many things. Yet, as I reflect back on our conversations over the last 20 years, I can't help but notice that we've spent most of our time talking about food! This common interest deepened as we both became wives and mothers with a passion for serving our husbands and children nourishing food.

We have both carried this love for healthy food into our work — me writing and teaching traditional cooking methods through TraditionalCookingSchool.com and authoring *The Complete Idiot's Guide to Fermenting Foods*, and Megan through blogging at EatBeautiful.net, teaching local cooking classes and opening Vanilla Jill's in Eugene, Oregon, with her husband, Tim. At this store, they offer Megan's signature, seasonally inspired, handmade, healthy low-sugar and no-sugar probiotic frozen treats. (And let's not forget the kombucha on tap and gut-healthy lunches, too!)

While I have always been a very good down-home and healthy cook, Megan made her mark on me (and my family) as a true food artist. She makes beautiful food — and she makes food beautiful. One year, our families vacationed together in the summer, and it happened to be my oldest daughter's birthday. We all (especially the birthday girl) still remember the amazing three-layer blueberry bars she created for the dessert!

At her house and restaurant, I have eaten some of the most scrumptious food ever. Broth-based soups bursting with flavor and goodness, and sandwiches on Paleo-friendly bread, stuffed with local raw cheese, pastured bacon, and veggies. (If you were to ask me what my favorite food is, I would say "a good sandwich" — and the best sandwiches I've ever had were made by Megan.) And desserts ... well, I already told you about the three-layer blueberry bars. The other delights I've tasted (ice creams, cakes, puddings and more) were just as amazing.

So it's truly not surprising to me that we are at this point — now lovingly unveiling Megan's first cookbook of beautiful, delicious, *healing* food. Welcome to *Eat Beautiful*.

I believe there's a purpose for everything in our lives. We can't choose what happens to us, but we can choose what we do. Even in the difficult times. Why do I mention this? Because Megan and her family have struggled (as perhaps you are doing right now) with food allergies, asthma, auto-immune diseases and more.

Megan never gave in to a life sentence of pharmaceuticals or a sub-par existence. Instead of giving up, she pushed for years to find answers, learning how to cook with limited allowable ingredients, and deeply immersing herself in healing diets and protocols. Megan chose to use her God-given gift of making food beautiful to solve a very real problem for her family — and to find healing.

You will read it soon in Megan's own words, but here's a hint at the results: Megan and her family are nearly fully healed. And, incredibly, on their healing journey with limited food choices, they've actually enjoyed eating! Is this really possible? Yes, it is. Megan does things with food I've never seen anyone else do. No matter what restrictive diet you're on — GAPS, AIP, Candida — you will find *scrumptious* healing recipes in this cookbook.

As you turn the pages and try the recipes in *Eat Beautiful*, I know you will feel and experience the same thing I did when I first met Megan: hope. Hope that your healing journey will end someday, and that along the way, the food you eat will deeply nourish your body, as well as thrill your soul (and your tastebuds) with its beauty.

—Wardee Harmon
founder of TraditionalCookingSchool.com
and author of *The Complete Idiot's Guide to Fermenting Foods*

ACKNOWLEDGEMENTS

*B*ehind every book published is a whole team of Very Important People, and *Eat Beautiful: Grain-free, Sugar-free and Loving It* is no exception. The following list of VIPs represents my team, and they deserve my unreserved thanks:

My husband, Timothy. You are a source of loving encouragement and support. I would never save you for last. You're the one who taught me to make perfect pie by being my go-to taste-tester — you looked so transported each time I succeeded. I get as much pleasure watching you devour (in three bites!) a cookie as you do while eating it. You have helped me carve out time to work, and you've always been supportive of my writing and kitchen endeavors. Your feedback has been the most valuable. And your hugs are to my tired soul what bone broth is to my belly. Now, let's go have a sunny vacation together!

Our children. I smile — and laugh — when I think about you tasting all of these recipes and many more. You ate more chocolate than most wise mamas would feed their kids for breakfast — but all for a good cause! We have enjoyed so many feasts together, and you have learned to appreciate good food and new flavors. You are the figs on my fruit tree, the ganache on my cake, the custard on my scone. You embellish my life. Your feedback reflects your maturity and discerning palates; it has been of huge practical help to me these past several years.

My Daddy, Jim Finney. You were my first cheerleader in the kitchen, and you remain one of my greatest advocates in every arena. Your wisdom and gracious way of giving advice make you a leader among men, as well as to your own grown-up children.

My Mommala, Susan Finney. You have shared your love of food with me in every possible way. Your encouragement of my blog and other endeavors with "comments" and childcare has been invaluable. Your love has been both practical and tender.

My Sister, Jilly. We've shared our lives — as I've served you cups of coffee and Paleo sandwiches — in the midst of our busyness and sometimes frail moments. These times amount to one of my life's greatest treasures.

Vanilla Jill's Scoops and Soups Cafe, located in the Whiteaker District in Eugene, Oregon.

Our Vanilla Jill's/Scoops and Soups customers — who are also our friends. So many of you have embarked on healing journeys similar to our own. We have experienced community with you as you have witnessed our hard work with a teeny budget and have cheered us on to success. My warm appreciation goes out to all of you who have encouraged us in our business enterprise and/or the production of this book. Specific warm hugs of thanks go to Susan Ralls, for believing in what I have to offer; Paul Baughman and Ally Roemer, for donating your time and photography skills, and for loving our vision and passion; Charlotte Dupont, for your huge, unexpected help late in the game, and for bringing along your good-naturedness, generosity and enthusiasm; Cindy Swanson, for your kindness and insights — you're a great teacher and entrepreneur; Kristy Peters and Emily Vogel, for your long friendship, which has been a source of encouragement and laughter for many years now; and Jason and Bernice Carbaugh, for your caring hearts and wise business counsel.

My dear friend Wardeh Harmon. You have encouraged me, both spiritually and professionally. I am grateful for your words that helped me believe in and persevere on this project.

My publishing team. Thanks to Sonya Hemmings, for your warmth, kindness and excellent editing; Heather Carraher, for beautiful cover and interior designs; and photographers George Filgate, Paul Baughman, Charlotte Dupont, Susan Ralls and Andrea Wyckoff of LowStarchPaleo.com, for your visual gifts and joyful spirits. It is my privilege to have worked with you.

My parents-in-law, Marshall and Kathleen Stevens. Your hearts have been intertwined with our success and, therefore, with the publication of this book. You have ceaselessly come alongside us with your generosity and assistance.

Finally, I thank every visitor to our stores (each one a VIP!) who has enjoyed our menu offerings and has eagerly awaited the publication of this cookbook. Now the recipes for your favorites — whether the Paleo Panini Roll, Pumpkin Cream Cheese Bar or Mixed-Berry Avocado Pie — are yours! I am grateful, too, for the hard-working food entrepreneurs and farmers who surround us. They have served as inspiring examples in our endeavor to bring healthy, slow food to our community.

INTRODUCTION

*I*n addition to being a mama who is devoted to our family's healing, I also teach GAPS, Paleo and WAP traditional-food cooking classes in Eugene, Oregon. I am also a Recipe Counselor, meeting each week with individuals who are referred to me by gastroenter-

ologists, naturopaths, energy practitioners and medical doctors. I am not a dietician or a nutritionist. My specialty is food, and healing food in particular. My goal when I meet with clients is to help them succeed on their healing diets. Too often patients receive a recommended diet from their healthcare practitioner but can't implement it for many reasons. I share recipes, techniques and practical inspiration to help my clients succeed and heal.

For four years, my husband Timothy and I have owned a frozen yogurt shop, Vanilla Jill's, in Eugene, Oregon, offering up handmade kefir-based and vegan frozen treats out of soft-serve machines we bought off eBay. The machines, which once churned trashy frozen yogurt mixes, now afford us the magic and privilege of serving healthy frozen desserts with pleasing texture and visual appeal.

Our experience has provided us with a blueprint for revolutionizing fast-food traditions. In the past two years, we have taken our vision even further, serving up savory foods that nourish and heal the body. Our third location, Scoops and Soups, has given us another link with our community, providing much-sought–after bone-broth-based soups and stews, as well as ice creams for every healthy eating lifestyle. Our career satisfaction grows as we welcome hungry bodies suffering from modern health epidemics, people who share our hope that many health problems can be healed by dietary changes.

A word we love is "alternatives." When you or a loved one has just been diagnosed with diabetes, autism, an autoimmune disease, celiac disease, leaky gut, asthma, ADD (Attention Deficit Disorder) or ADHD (Attention Deficit Hyperactivity Disorder), IBS (Irritable Bowel Syndrome), SIBO (Small Intestine Bacterial Overgrowth), candida overgrowth or food allergies, you need new foods — more nutritious and just as delicious — to replace the old favorites.

My family, too, is on its own journey of healing. Our passion for eating well was born out of our own health adversities — trials I no longer regret! Healing our bodies of asthma, candida overgrowth, autoimmune diseases and more has spurred us to seek a new way of eating and living that is actually more satisfying than our previous, conventional American diet and lifestyle. We sit down to feasts three times a day. We delight in the cooking process. We have developed lots of easy and fast recipes. And we feel the difference in our bodies every meal, every day. We said goodbye to the symptoms we had experienced, and over time we have been rewarded with efficient digestion and a big picture of hope and healing.

All of this encouragement and enlightenment can be served up to you, too, in the form of savory-cobbler meat and vegetable pies, delightful sweet or savory waffles, perfect chocolate cake, ice cream (dairy-free options abound!), pies, cookies, scones and more. I have filled these pages with years of recipe research and customer-tested favorites. I have taught cooking classes for years and have shared student favorites. And each recipe is packed with possibilities and variations, because many readers may have food allergies that can be limiting. An ice cream made with homemade cashew milk can be substituted with sprouted pine nut milk or the economical and easy-to-make (or buy) coconut milk. I give you not just one recipe for chocolate frosting, but three. And there are four different chocolate chip cookie recipes! Sometimes recipe variations call for completely different sweeteners to meet various readers' needs. Other recipes might be nut-free or egg-free — and yet they all taste indulgent and delicious. Many recipes reflect the comfort foods we long for, but in healthier versions, like Pumpkin Pie or Blueberry Muffins. Others put a twist on traditional flavors by marrying them with revolutionary

changes that surprise and delight the palate, such as Chocolate Cake made with grated beets or zucchini and spread with Avocado-Hemp Chocolate Fudge Ganache, or Pizza Dough topped with veggies, sausage, and Dairy-free Nut Cheese. Some ingredients may be difficult to access outside of urban areas, but I have put the greatest emphasis on making recipes that are accessible to everyone, wherever you may live, by providing substitutions and resources for ordering hard-to-find items.

The intention of this book is to impart a new passion in the kitchen to my readers and to provide solutions for those who are overwhelmed by new dietary restrictions. I have kept the recipes simple and basic, with just the right amount of guidance to steer you to success. After all, the best food is often the simplest: whole foods grown naturally and in season, prepared easily but thoughtfully. And surprisingly, the techniques used to make grain-free baked goods are often easier than those required by modern baking recipes. I hope readers will embrace these recipes out of a love of eating and a desire to be healed or to become healthier. Whether we realize it or not, we all hunger to get back to the way we are designed to eat: no processed foods, foods grown locally, foods that are "predigested" (which I'll discuss later in further detail; see Appendix 2: Methods, Page 270). It's my hope that these recipes will teach you to cook in a way that combines the wisdom of the past with the knowledge of the present day.

One thing that makes this cookbook unique from other grain-free recipe books is the lack of dependence on ingredients like coconut flour and almond flour. I have spent two years learning and creating baking techniques that are healthier and more true to the flavor and texture of classic baked goods but without the added starches and nut-based flours and butters that are often used in grain-free baked goods. While many recipes that call for almond butter or tapioca starch taste good, these ingredients are not healthful or ideal for healing diets. (I discuss the quality of almonds and almond products later on in the book. See Glossary of Ingredients, Chapter 13, Page 256) And for the record I do like coconut flour when it is used sparingly, but I am not one to say it is high in nutrition. Factory-made coconut flours have little coconut essence remaining. But this ingredient is a good tool in certain recipes to create the right texture. (I expound upon the uses of coconut flour later on, as well. See Glossary of Ingredients, Chapter 13, Page 257)

The chocolate chip cookies featured in this cookbook taste like the classic version — the ones made with white flour. My husband, the ultimate cookie lover, has really enjoyed the test batches. And that is my goal: to give you recipes you'll return to again and again — and as an essential bonus, for them to be healthier than their conventional counterparts, made from nutrients that are easy to digest without taxing your body.

Lastly, it has been my goal to do for you what Molly Katzen's book *The Enchanted Broccoli Forest* did for me almost twenty years ago, when I was a new wife. I want to share with you how to bake (in this case grain-free), by showing you how ingredients work in recipes and what combinations go well together. For experimental cooks who want to create their own healthy recipes, this book will teach you basic techniques and patterns that will guide you. For those who prefer the tried and true, this book will become your reliable answer, allowing you to make perfect chocolate cake, dreamy dairy-free Crème Anglaise, and brownies that both you and the kids will love.

If you are making a change to heal yourself or someone you love, I salute you for your efforts to improve your health. Some open-mindedness, courage and a willingness to embark on an adventure are necessary. I promise that your body will quickly feel the change. You will notice a difference, and the foods you eat will bring you pleasure! For those of you just looking for better-tasting recipes, I am so happy to share this collection of family favorites with you. Cheers! And thanks for supporting the work I love to do.

Warmly and with hope,
Megan Stevens

For more great recipes and nutritional insights, check out my blog, Eat Beautiful (www.eatbeautiful.net), and my Eat Beautiful Facebook page.

A FRAMEWORK OF DIETS

Where are you in your health journey? To borrow a Dr. Seuss-style phrase, I'm about 97 and 3/4 percent along my particular path. We all know that life is about the journey and not the destination, but when it comes to healing, we do want to arrive. But what does arriving look like?

Arriving for me will mean being symptom-free and being able to maintain a whole-food, slow-food diet — omitting many foods because of their toxic effects. In the meantime, as I strive to get where I'm going, I've been grateful to find that the most healing diets also keep me satisfied.

I have used three healing diets as the framework for this cookbook:

- The Gut and Psychology Syndrome (GAPS) Diet
- The Weston A. Price Diet
- The Paleo/Autoimmune Protocol (AIP) Diet

What follows are explanations and explorations of each of these diets — with many intertwined elements — which have helped so many to heal.

The Gut and Psychology Syndrome Diet, well-known by its acronym GAPS, is probably the most strict of these three diets. Its list of foods to avoid is the longest, but the short story is one of success. Developed by British physician Dr. Natasha Campbell-McBride, GAPS stems from scientific research that shows a significant link between the health of the gut and the health of the brain. Since originating this diet, Dr. Campbell-McBride has aided many families, including her own.

At its core, GAPS is a modification to the Specific Carbohydrate Diet, an effective eating plan that is helping thousands of people find relief from colitis, Crohn's disease and celiac disease. Dr. Campbell-McBride made some essential changes to the SCD that she observed would more broadly address gut-brain disorders (including attention-deficit disorders, Asperger's syndrome and autism spectrum disorders), as well as gastro-intestinal symptoms and autoimmune diseases. Her book, simply titled *Gut and Psychology Syndrome*, details the science that supports her research, and her companion cookbook, *Internal Bliss*, provides a practical outline for implementing the diet for those who might benefit most. In addition to foods that should be avoided, she focuses on the nutrient-dense foods that should be eaten to restore and maintain gut health. The purpose of the GAPS Diet is to heal a condition called leaky gut syndrome, which often leads to pathogen overgrowth. This conditions is most often diagnosed by naturopaths, but occasionally by medical doctors, too. By starving pathogens of all sugars and starches and healing the mucosal lining of the gut — largely with bone broths and regular amounts of fermented foods — the diet restores the gut's proper flora balance and also heals whatever disease symptoms might have resulted from an underlying condition, including diabetes, irritable bowel syndrome, interstitial cystitis, asthma, dyslexia, food allergies and many others.

The plan consists of eating only homemade whole foods and following a starch- and sugar-free diet without exception. Cheating sabotages the process. This is a diet for a sick person who is determined to get well. It works, but it's work. I have been on the diet for four years, and I actually enjoy the stage I've reached. The introductory stage — affectionately known as just "Intro" among devotees — is dramatically effective. (I am currently working on a wonderful soup cookbook for the introductory GAPS Diet, containing recipes that are so yummy my family did not mind the diet's initial limits.) In my opinion, the GAPS Diet is challenging but effective, and worth the sacrifices required.

The Weston A. Price Diet, also referred to as a Traditional diet, exists in a continuous circle with the GAPS Diet. Many start and finish with the Weston A. Price Diet, stopping to do the GAPS Diet along the way out of necessity. This diet emphasizes the critical importance of traditionally raised and prepared foods —meat, milk and butter from grass-fed cattle; fermented cod liver oil and other fermented foods, including grains, vegetables and fruits; organic produce; and properly prepared (by soaking or sprouting) nuts and seeds. Because the diet's goal is excellent general health for the average person, there is no need to exclude starches or grains. Raw and living enzymes and saturated fats are also emphasized. Sally Fallon's book *Nourishing Traditions* provides a well-researched education about why these particular foods have been found to be the most healthful, as does the Weston A. Price website.

The Paleo Diet reaches a different demographic with a similar, but evolving, message. Strict guidelines were first taught by the Paleo Diet's orginator, Dr. Loren Cordain, but I like that it is a diet of inclusiveness and tolerance, meaning people can commit to it as much as they are able. More importantly, I like how it has changed over time to become, in my opinion, more accurate and supporting to the body's functions.

To be specific, the original Paleo Diet emphasized lean meat — grass-fed, but low-fat. I don't believe that low-fat diets benefit our systems. Good grass-fed or saturated fats help so many functions in our body. But most Paleo proponents don't adhere to this original low-fat stipulation at all. In fact, bacon is a ubiquitous ingredient in most Paleo cookbooks. Coconut oil, coconut milk, nuts and other high-fat nourishing foods are also ever-present. Cordain originally put no emphasis on organ meats, but now many Paleo recipes incorporate this healthful food, using the whole animal for the good of all involved.

Cordain has reached masses with his teaching, making good health, weight loss and healing attainable to tens of thousands who might never have heard of the Weston A. Price or GAPS diets. The movement teaches a grain-free, no-sugar diet. While I feel that fermented or pre-digested grains can be a fine choice for those who are healthy, eliminating grains inarguably helps to heal the sick. Most Americans who are slowly dropping into disease and malnourishment, consuming genetically modified organisms produced by Monsanto and eating factory-made food, would find Paleo a much better diet choice. As with the GAPS Diet, someone starting the Paleo Diet to get well will find a grain-free diet is an essential piece of the puzzle. The Paleo Diet is also one of whole foods, grass-fed meats and organic veggies. The one thing to avoid? Paleo baking recipes that use starches such as conventional potato flour and tapioca or store-bought nut butters to create the right texture. Watch out for these ingredients. They are not Paleo in spirit, and they are difficult to digest if you need to be on a healing diet. (I mean no offense to those who have created these recipes. They are indeed innovative — just not as healthy as they might seem.)

The Autoimmune Protocol (AIP) is the healing branch of the Paleo Diet. As implied, it is designed specifically for those Paleo eaters who are trying to put their autoimmune diseases into remission. I have seen in my recipe counseling practice that the GAPS Diet is not ideal for all bodies. For instance, those with histamine allergies cannot handle bone broth or fermented foods, but they often do fine with sweet potatoes, (which are not allowed on GAPS). Diets for healing are not one-size-fits-all. AIP also does not allow for nuts, while GAPS does. This cookbook takes these variations into account, offering many recipes without nuts, as well as many with sprouted nuts. (I have designated all AIP recipes in Appendix 3 so they are easy to locate.) The AIP version of the Paleo Diet is excellent, and I strongly recommend it for certain individuals.

Two other diets complement the previously mentioned three:

- The Low-Fermentable, Oligo-, Di-, Mono-saccharides and Polyols (FODMAP) Diet
- The Anti-Candida Diet

Both of these diets also embrace sugar-free principles that help the body heal itself. They overlap with the aforementioned diets because they all are working to heal similar conditions. The Low-FODMAP Diet works specifically to relieve the symptoms associated with Irritable Bowel Syndrome. I have personally experienced relief from bloating by following the guidelines of the diet, which removes foods like onions, avocados, xylitol and winter squash, which, in certain people, ferment and cause gas, bloating and other uncomfortable symptoms. This diet can be done in conjunction with the GAPS Diet with great success. I have written online about how to pursue these two diets together for synergistic healing (please see http://eatbeautiful.net/2014/03/26/low-fodmap-gaps-combination-diet-healing-ibs-pathogen-overgrowth-and-sibo/)".

The Anti-Candida Diet is very similar to the GAPS Diet. It is aggressive, restrictive and healing. Individuals who adhere to this diet remove not only all of the foods that GAPS adherents remove, but also additional foods that can exacerbate pathogen overgrowth, such as mushrooms, peanut butter and cheese. Some suggest removing vegetables with fructose, like carrots and beets. I have personally used this diet and found it to be helpful.

Sprouted macadamia nuts.

For the purposes of this cookbook, it is important to see that these diets emphasize either no grains and no sugar for healing the gut and thus the entire body, or predigested grains and an education about how and which "sugars" to consume for the maintenance of a healthy body. Even people who are able to maintain good health on a Traditional diet will be grateful for the grain-free, sugar-free recipes in this book. The techniques in my recipes help your body utilize the nutrients of some of the most beneficial foods. The ingredients are gentle on sensitive digestion systems, and tremendous health advantages come in the form of a treat. None of us needs ever again to revert to the banana bread and brownie recipes we grew up with. Why? The recipes in this book are better for you (by a mile!) and will leave you feeling satisfied and healthy instead of indulged and wanting more. At the end of the day, we needn't sorrow over having to say goodbye to old favorites. Instead, we need to recognize them for the sugar-laden recipes they are and be grateful that they appeared in our lives for only awhile. Let's now intervene and redefine our favorites. Let's teach our children the traditional wisdom of easy practices like soaking and sprouting.

We are grateful for these modern, science-based diets: GAPS, Weston A. Price, and Paleo/AIP. Together, they provide a roadmap that guides us back to ancient traditions. May one or all of these diets — along with the recipes in this cookbook that celebrate them — help you to enjoy a whole new relationship with food.

waffles, pancakes and crepes

CHAPTER ONE

Waffles, Pancakes and Crepes

When these morning favorites hit the table, breakfast becomes alive and interactive. Toppings are invited to the party. Two toppings offer options. Three or more suggest a Lazy Susan — lots of passing, spooning and fun. Waffles, pancakes and crepes are about coming together for a decadent meal — savory or sweet, and surprisingly special. These are the moments we look for in life.

WAFFLE #1

"Carrot Cake"

(grain-free, stevia-sweetened)

Here's just one of many reasons to get a juicer: You can turn leftover carrot pulp into flour that helps build the batter for these waffles. No more gluten-free mixes! This is a recipe full of nutrition, natural sweetness and healthy fats that will satisfy your appetite and make you smile. These waffles are also easy to eat out-of-hand, like muffins.

10 eggs, preferably grass-fed

3/4 cup dates, cut into pieces no larger than 1 inch

1 ripe banana

1 cup melted, grass-fed ghee or butter (or coconut oil), slightly cooled

1 cup sprouted homemade almond/other nut butter* (See Appendix 2: Methods). Or for a nut-free variation, use 1 cup coconut butter.

1/2 cup carrot flour (recipe follows), or substitute 1/2 cup chopped, raw carrots + 1/2 cup coconut flour

1 teaspoon cinnamon

1/8 teaspoon sea salt

1/16 teaspoon powdered stevia (or 10 to 15 drops liquid stevia — NuNaturals brand preferred)

coconut oil spray (optional; see Alternative High-Heat Fats on Page 272)

Yields approximately 8 waffles.

1. Grease waffle iron with coconut spray or alternative, and preheat it to medium heat.

2. Place all ingredients in a high-powered blender, in the order listed.

3. Puree on medium speed until smooth, stopping the motor once to scrape down the sides and then proceeding until the batter is smooth and uniformly mixed — about 50 seconds total.

4. Pour the batter into the waffle iron and cook according to manufacturer's instructions. (If you have a Belgian waffle iron, pour or ladle 1/3 to 1/2 cup batter per quadrant, using 2 cups total per batch.)

5. Serve with butter, fruit, sweetened yogurt/sour cream/frozen yogurt and syrup, or honey, as desired. Or eat plain, as a snack.

Because most commercially made almond butters are rancid and the almonds aren't sprouted, it is best to make your own from soaked and dehydrated almonds. The health benefits make it worth the effort! See How to Make Almond (or Other Nut) Butter on Page 271.

carrot flour

Equipment needed: low/no-heat extraction juicer

15 to 20 carrots, depending on size

Yields about 2 cups.

1. Juice carrots.
2. Enjoy the juice within 30 minutes for optimum nutrition.
3. Save the pulp!
4. Line your dehydrator with cheesecloth, a fine-mesh screen that fits the dehydrator's shape, or a large square of parchment paper, cutting an "x" in the middle of it for center-ventilated circular machines.
5. Spread the carrot pulp over the surface, keeping some of it intact in small clumps.
6. Dehydrate the pulp at desired heat (115 degrees is average) until fully dry, about 24 hours.
7. Using a large bowl (or clean pillowcase) to catch all the pieces, empty the pulp into the bowl. Use your fingers to get all the dry pieces that may stick.
8. Place all the dried pulp into a high-powered blender and blend on medium speed until the pulp has become powdered, about 30 seconds.
9. The "flour" is now ready for use in the above waffle recipe. You will have some left over. It can also be sealed in a storage container and used at a later date.

WAFFLE #2

"Yellow Cake"

(nut-free, stevia-sweetened)

Although I don't usually like to rely on coconut flour exclusively for the bread-y texture in baked goods, this recipe is mostly made from grass-fed eggs and is, therefore, a lovely culinary trick. The coconut flour is a tool, used in small measure, and is especially helpful if you are nut-free. And these waffles are fun because they are reminiscent of yellow cake. However, not only are they high in protein, good fatty acids, and beta-carotene, they don't need baking soda. This a bonus for those on healing diets, such as the GAPS Diet, because baking soda makes the stomach more alkaline. Those with digestion issues need proper stomach acidity for optimum digestion. This recipe is extra yummy if you can tolerate butter or ghee, but it is still nice made with coconut oil.

8 eggs, preferably grass-fed

3/4 cup melted grass-fed ghee or butter (or coconut oil), slightly cooled

1/2 cup coconut flour

1/2 cup unsweetened applesauce (use homemade fresh applesauce from peeled Granny Smith apples, if fructose/sugar sensitive; recipe follows)

1/8 teaspoon sea salt

1/16 teaspoon powdered stevia, or 10 to 15 drops liquid stevia (NuNaturals brand preferred)

coconut oil spray (optional; see Alternative High-Heat Fats on Page 272)

Yields approximately 8 waffles.

1. Grease waffle iron with coconut oil spray and preheat it to medium-high heat.
2. Place all ingredients in a high-powdered blender and puree until smooth, stopping to scrape down the sides once with a rubber spatula, as necessary.
3. Pour the batter into the waffle iron and cook according to manufacturer's instructions. (If you have a Belgian waffle iron, pour or ladle about a 1/2 cup batter per quadrant, using 2 cups total per batch.)
4. Top with homemade Granny Smith applesauce or your favorite toppings.

Variations:

- replace applesauce with 1/2 cup mashed banana
- replace applesauce with 1/2 cup steamed and pureed carrots or zucchini
- replace applesauce with 1/2 cup cooked winter squash

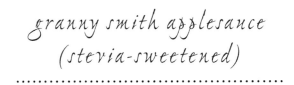

granny smith applesauce (stevia-sweetened)

2 large or 4 small Granny Smith apples, peeled and chopped into 1-inch cubes or 1/2-inch slices

3/4 cup water

1/16 teaspoon powdered stevia, or 8 drops liquid stevia (NuNaturals brand preferred)

Yields 1-½ cups.

1. Place all ingredients in a small to medium-size saucepan.
2. Cover saucepan.
3. Over low heat, simmer apples until tender and water has mostly evaporated, watching carefully to avoid any scorching — about 10 to 15 minutes.
4. Use in any recipe that calls for applesauce, or serve as a topping.

WAFFLE #3

Sprouted Nut

(stevia-sweetened)

2 cups raw, soaked and sprouted wet (See Appendix 2: Methods) nuts of choice (if using almonds, use only 1-3/4 cups)

8 eggs, preferably grass-fed

3/4 cup ghee or coconut oil, melted and cooled

1/4 teaspoon sea salt

1/8 teaspoon powdered stevia, or 15 to 20 drops liquid stevia (NuNaturals brand preferred)

1/2 teaspoon baking soda, sifted (optional; omit for those with stomach pH sensitivity)

1/3 cup flaxseed meal

1/4 cup chia seeds

coconut oil spray (optional; see Alternative High-Heat Fats on Page 272)

Yields about 9 waffles.

1. Place first 5 ingredients in a high-powered blender and puree until smooth, about 50 seconds on medium-high speed for most blenders.
2. Start the blender again on medium-low speed and, opening the small insert in the lid, add baking soda all at once.
3. Quickly add flaxseed meal and chia seeds, and blend for an additional 10 seconds. Do not over-blend.

4. Allow the batter to set up and thicken for 10 minutes while you grease and preheat waffle iron to medium-high heat.

5. Pour batter into waffle iron and cook according to manufacturer's instructions. (If you have a Belgian waffle iron, pour or ladle about 1/2 cup batter per quadrant, using 2 cups total per batch.)

6. Cool waffles on a metal cooling rack or on paper bags cut open and spread out. Reheat as needed in a toaster or oven. Waffles keep well in the freezer, wrapped in parchment paper and placed in a sealed container.

Add-ins and variations:

- 1-1/2 cups diced Granny Smith apples (unpeeled is OK) or berries can be folded in at the end just before the batter sets up and thickens. When baking, use extra grease on the waffle iron to prevent sticking.

- 1 cup soaked and dehydrated whole or chopped nuts can be folded in at the end just before the batter sets up and thickens.

- 1/2 cup unsweetened shaved chocolate or nibs, can be folded in at the end just before the batter sets up and thickens.

- Optional spices: 2 teaspoons cinnamon, 1 teaspoon ginger, 1/2 teaspoon cloves or allspice, and 1 teaspoon vanilla, can be added with the original 5 ingredients and blended well.

- 1/3 cup cocoa powder can be added with the original 5 ingredients and blended well.

- 1/2 cup cooked winter squash or pumpkin can be added with the original 5 ingredients and blended well.

WAFFLE #4

Chocolate Chia Seed

(nut-free, stevia-sweetened)

The combination of cocoa and chia seeds creates a yeast-like texture. The flavor is versatile and can go toward savory or sweet: Eat them with soup, like a side of toast with butter, or top them with all your favorite sweet waffle toppings for a traditional waffle preparation. This recipe is a personal favorite.

8 eggs, preferably grass-fed

3/4 cup chia seeds

3/4 cup extra-virgin olive oil, coconut oil or preferred fat, melted and cooled

1/3 cup fair-trade cocoa

2 teaspoons vanilla

1/4 teaspoon sea salt

1/8 teaspoon powdered stevia, or 15 to 20 drops liquid stevia (NuNaturals brand preferred)

1 teaspoon water

1/2 teaspoon baking soda

1. Add first 7 ingredients to a high-powered blender.
2. Process on medium-low speed for 30 seconds. Keep blender motor going as you proceed with the next step.
3. Swirl the baking soda and water together well with your finger immediately before pouring into blender. Pour them in.
4. Process 5 seconds more. Stop motor. Allow batter to set up and thicken for 10 to 15 minutes.
5. Pour batter in scant 1/2 cup amounts into your waffle iron and cook according to the manufacturer's instructions.
6. Top with cultured cream and berries, homemade ice cream and sprouted walnuts, or butter and aged cheese.

Macadamia Nut Pancakes with Coconut Syrup

(stevia-sweetened)

1 cup raw macadamia nuts, soaked and wet (see Appendix 2: Methods)

8 eggs, preferably grass-fed

3/4 cup ghee or coconut oil, melted and cooled

1/2 cup flaxseed meal

1/4 teaspoon sea salt

1/8 teaspoon powdered stevia, or 15 to 20 drops liquid stevia (NuNaturals brand preferred)

2 tablespoons coconut flour

1/2 teaspoon baking soda

ghee, duck fat or coconut oil

1. If you plan to serve the pancakes with homemade coconut syrup (recipe follows), make the syrup first, as it needs to chill slightly before being served.
2. For the pancake batter, place the first 6 ingredients in the blender and puree until smooth, about 50 seconds on medium-high speed for most blenders.

3. Sift together the baking soda and coconut flour. Start the blender again on medium-low speed and, opening the small insert in the lid, add the baking soda and coconut flour all at once and blend for an additional 10 seconds. Do not over-blend.

4. Cook the pancakes over medium-low heat, choosing their size according to your preference.

5. Each pancake is ready to be flipped when the sides are dried out and small holes and bubbles are just starting to form in the center of each pancake. Continue this process until all of the batter is used, adding more fat to the pan as needed.

6. Keep pancakes warm on a plate in a 200-degree-Fahrenheit oven until ready to serve.

7. Serve the pancakes with optional coconut syrup, chopped, "crispy" macadamia nuts or walnuts, and other favorite pancake toppings: fresh fruit, compote, lightly sweetened crème fraiche or yogurt, or maple syrup.

Coconut Syrup

1 cup hot water

2/3 cup unsweetened dried coconut

1/2 cup organic maple syrup, local raw honey, coconut sugar or hardwood-derived xylitol

1/3 cup coconut oil, ghee or butter

1 teaspoon vanilla

1/2 teaspoon sustainably sourced gelatin

1. Place all ingredients in a high-powered blender and blend on medium-high speed for about 1 minute.
2. Pour the syrup through a fine mesh strainer into a small to medium-size bowl, pressing on the coconut solids to extract all of the liquid.
3. Chill the syrup in the refrigerator, stirring it occasionally, until the pancakes are ready.
4. Serve the syrup chilled, as the gelatin thickens as it cools, creating a pleasantly viscous texture that will become runnier when it hits the hot pancakes.

AIP Pancakes

(egg-free, nut-free)

2 whole plantains, black or close to black in color, fully ripe

1/4 cup coconut oil, melted

1/4 cup cricket flour*(see Resources for suppliers), or substitute with coconut flour if you prefer

3 tablespoons filtered water

2 teaspoons sustainably sourced gelatin

1 teaspoon cinnamon

optional: scant powdered stevia (NuNaturals brand preferred), or 1 tablespoon honey

1. Place the water and melted coconut oil into blender.
2. Add the peeled plantains and all remaining ingredients.
3. Blend on low speed until the puree is smooth, 30 to 50 seconds, using the pulse button or scraping down the sides as needed.
4. Melt 1 tablespoon coconut oil in a hot cast-iron skillet and pour in the first batch of batter in rounds, turning the heat to medium-low once the batter is poured in.

5. Allow the edges to dry out a bit and some bubbles to form, as you would with traditional pancakes, then flip and cook on the second side.

6. Proceed in this manner until all the batter is cooked, keeping the first batch warm in a 200-degree oven until ready to serve. Garnish as desired. (I garnished the above pictured pancakes with lightly sweetened coconut butter.)

Recipe Notes

This recipe makes 7 to 8 medium-size pancakes. It can serve 3 to 4 people if you have side dishes of meat and condiments. If you want a big plate of pancakes for each person, then this recipe will serve 2. The recipe can be doubled.

*Crickets produce fewer greenhouse gases than conventional beef and can be raised on less land. They are high in protein, good fats, calcium, iron, zinc and B vitamins — everything you'd hope for when eating any meat source. About 80 percent of the world's population consumes insects. But to Americans, it is taboo.

Yet with concerns about poor animal husbandry principles and its ill effects on land, air and ozone, increasing numbers of radical foodies are making this dietary change to benefit the planet. The goal is to reduce one's carbon footprint — not by going vegan or vegetarian, (because our bodies are obviously omnivorous by design), but by eating insects. For me and many other grain-free foodies who have allergies, there is an additional benefit to using cricket flour. I try to limit my nut consumption, and I am allergic to coconut flour (which is great, but has its limitations). Cricket flour is a new flour replacement, providing nutritional variety in our diet as well as the functional favor of filling in for other flour substitutes. While none of us should have too many nuts, in a diet of implicit moderation cricket flour is hard to overdo. I love cricket flour because as a meat source, it is a complete protein (unlike other grain-free flour substitutes) and contains all of the essential amino acids. So what does it taste like? Its flavor resembles that of buckwheat. It's got a seed-like quality that is complex and delicious!

Crepes

This recipe came to me suddenly, as if from the heavens. And I'm grateful it did. I grew up eating blintzes every Christmas, with a Jewish mama who brought her riches to create a new family tradition. My sister Jill and I simply can't bear a Christmas without them. And this recipe has brought back that possibility, so that our children can know the authentic experience and lacey pleasure of crepes—without the gluten and sugar. As with all crepe recipes, remember that the first crepe functions to season the pan. It will be ugly and a treat for the cook to nibble on. All the others will turn out beautifully.

2/3 cup homemade vegan milk (recipe follows) or raw dairy milk

1/4 cup coconut oil, grass-fed ghee or butter, melted and cooled slightly

4 eggs, preferably grass-fed

1/4 teaspoon sea salt

1/16 teaspoon powdered stevia (or 5 to 8 drops liquid stevia — NuNaturals brand preferred — or 2 teaspoons honey, if tolerated)

1/4 cup walnuts, soaked, sprouted and dehydrated

2 tablespoons coconut flour

1 tablespoon flaxseed meal

1 teaspoon chia seeds

Serves 3 to 4. This recipe doubles well.

1. Place all ingredients in a blender in the order they are listed, and puree until smooth.
2. Set aside the batter for 10 minutes, during which time it will thicken.
3. Melt a tablespoon of coconut oil or ghee in a small or medium-size hot skillet, preferably cast-iron.
4. Pour about 1/4 cup of the batter into the pan, depending on the pan's size, making a thin layer of batter cover the bottom by turning and rotating the pan. Cook until the batter is bubbly, less wet and cooked around the edges, browning and beginning to peel up.
5. Flip the crepe using a fork (to lift the sides) and your fingers, or use a spatula without scraping the bottom of the pan. (You want to keep the "nonstick" surface only touched by the crepes themselves, which helps it stay "nonstick.")
6. Cook the other side briefly, 10 to 30 seconds.
7. These are delicious served with some of our favorite fillings:
   - Homemade compote or berries on top and custard inside (see recipes on Pages 188, 199)
   - Homemade sprouted peanut butter or almond butter, (see Appendix 2: Methods), honey, and sliced bananas. Add dark chocolate (vegan) ice cream (see recipe on Page 194) for a fantasy breakfast!
   - Traditional blintz fillings, such as Fully Cultured Sweet Cheese topped with Raw Jam and Granny Smith Applesauce (16, 201)
   - Scrambled eggs and cheese, with sautéed onions and bell peppers, plus a side of bacon!
   - Sautéed mushrooms, fresh tarragon, homemade gravy (use bone broth to deglaze drippings from a baked chicken!), caramelized onions and sausage
   - Ratatouille of summer zucchini, eggplant, peppers, onions, garlic and olive oil
   - Leftover shredded roast chicken, homemade pesto, fresh veggies such as garden tomatoes, cucumbers, and a favorite aged cheese: brie, gouda, jack or a vegan Herbed Dairy-free Ricotta (163)
   - Mashed sweet potatoes, mashed baked winter squash, or mashed, cooked rutabaga/turnip, topped with sharp cheese and melted; add bacon pieces, and sautéed green onions

Homemade Hemp or Nut Milk

Combine in a high-powered blender: 3 cups filtered water and 2/3 cup raw hemp seeds (or a sprouted wet nut or seed of your choice). Add 1/16 teaspoons powdered stevia (or 5 to 8 drops liquid stevia). Process on medium-high speed for 50 seconds. Do not strain. The milk is now ready to use.

scones & scuffins

CHAPTER TWO

Scones and Scuffins

Pleasure comes from perfect texture, the breaking of something buttery, the crumble and chew, the mouth-feel, and rich, satisfying fat. I am an instant hedonist with a scone in my mouth. Enjoy again that traditional British experience and humbler versions of the same.

Traditional Scones

(stevia-sweetened)

2 cups cashews, soaked and wet (see Appendix 2: Methods)

4 eggs, preferably grass-fed

1/2 cup coconut oil, very cold from the refrigerator

1/4 teaspoon sea salt

1/8 teaspoon powdered stevia (or 15 drops liquid stevia — NuNaturals brand preferred)

1/2 cup coconut flour

1/2 teaspoon baking soda

1-1/2 cups frozen berries, blueberries or blackberries preferred

Yields 6 scones.

Preheat oven to 325 degrees Fahrenheit.

1. Lightly grease 2 baking sheets or line them with parchment paper, and set aside. (Coconut oil spray can be a good tool for this step.) Make sure the baking sheet you choose has an edge or rim at least 1 inch high, as some of the fat may melt and run out.
2. Scoop the cold coconut oil onto a cutting board. Cut it into very small pieces, no piece bigger than a pea.
3. Place the small cold pieces of coconut oil onto a plate lined with parchment or wax paper and place this plate back into the refrigerator.

4. Place cashews, eggs, sea salt and stevia into the work bowl of a food processor. Process until the cashews are mostly pureed, about 60 to 90 seconds.
5. Sift together the coconut flour and baking soda.
6. Add the frozen coconut oil pieces and the dry ingredients to the cashew puree in the food processor. Pulse to mostly combine, about 8 to 10 pulses.
7. Add the frozen berries and pulse to combine again briefly, being very careful not to cut the berries too small or to over-mix the dough.
8. Dump the dough out onto a large flat surface, (a marble surface is ideal because it stays cold and keeps the dough cold), but even a large wooden cutting board will work fine.
9. Create a large flat circle with your hands. Pat and mold the dough into this shape, careful not to over-work it. The circle should be approximately 1-1/2 inches thick and about 8 inches in diameter.
10. Cut the circle in half, then each half into thirds, creating 6 pie-shaped wedges total.
11. Place the wedges on the prepared baking sheet.
12. Bake 30 to 35 minutes, until golden brown and firm to the touch. Remove from the oven and allow to cool for 5 minutes before transferring to a cooling rack or serving.

Variations:

- Substitute frozen diced pieces of Granny Smith apple for the berries, adding 1 teaspoon cinnamon.

Almond-Blueberry Scones

(stevia-sweetened)

Few things in life afford me as much pleasure as hearing a member of my family cooing over something I've baked. These are my 11-year-old son's favorite, and I, therefore, love serving them. They are the hippy-healthy version of a scone — chewy and crumbly, with all the sweetness coming from the blueberries.

2 cups almonds, soaked and wet (see Appendix 2: Methods)

2 eggs, preferably grass-fed

1/3 cup coconut oil, very cold from the refrigerator

1 teaspoon vanilla

1/8 teaspoon powdered stevia (or 15 drops liquid stevia — NuNaturals brand preferred)

1/4 teaspoon sea salt

1/3 cup coconut flour

1/2 teaspoon baking soda

1-1/2 cups frozen blueberries

Yields 6 scones.

Preheat oven to 325 degrees Fahrenheit.

1. Lightly grease a baking sheet or line it with parchment paper, and set aside. (Coconut oil spray can be a good tool for this step.) Make sure the baking sheet you choose has an edge or rim at least 1 inch high, as some of the fat may melt and run out.

2. Scoop the cold coconut oil onto a cutting board. With a large knife, cut the chunk of oil into very small pieces, no piece bigger than a pea.

3. Place the small cold pieces of coconut oil onto a plate lined with parchment or wax paper; and put the plate back into the refrigerator.

4. Place almonds, eggs, vanilla, sea salt and stevia into the work bowl of a food processor. Process until the almonds are mostly pureed, about 60 to 90 seconds. Scrape down the sides of the work bowl.

5. Sift together the coconut flour and baking soda.

6. Add the frozen coconut oil pieces and the dry ingredients to the almond puree in the food processor. Pulse to mostly combine, about 8 to 10 pulses.

7. Add the frozen berries and pulse to combine briefly, being careful not to cut the berries too small, or to over-mix the dough.

8. Dump the dough out onto a large flat surface, (a marble surface is ideal because it stays cold and keeps the dough cold), but even a large wooden cutting board will work fine.

9. Create a large flat circle with your hands. Pat and mold the dough into this shape, careful not to over-work it. The circle should be approximately 1-1/2 inches thick and about 8 inches in diameter.

10. Cut the circle in half, then each half into thirds, creating 6 pie-shaped wedges total.

11. Place the wedges on the prepared baking sheet, using an offset metal spatula.

12. Bake 30 to 35 minutes, until golden brown and firm to the touch. Remove from the oven and allow them to cool for 5 minutes before transferring to a cooling rack or serving.

Cashew-Blueberry Scuffins

(stevia-sweetened)

My kids insist that no name but scuffins will do for what they consider the finest in dessert-like breakfast foods. This batter is designed to be in the shape of a drop scone or loose biscuit but to have the texture of a muffin or enriched dough.

2 cups cashews, soaked and wet (see Appendix 2: Methods)

6 eggs, grass-fed preferred

3/4 cup extra-virgin olive oil

1/4 teaspoon sea salt

1/8 teaspoon + a teeny bit more powdered stevia (or 15 to 20 drops liquid stevia — NuNaturals brand preferred)

1/2 cup flaxseed meal

1/3 cup chia seeds, processed into a meal in a high-powered blender or coffee grinder

1/2 teaspoon baking soda

3/4 cup frozen blueberries

3/4 cup cashew pieces, sprouted and wet, or dehydrated

Yields 8 scuffins.

Preheat oven to 325 degrees Fahrenheit.

1. Lightly grease 2 baking sheets or line them with parchment paper, and set aside. (Coconut oil spray can be a good tool for this step.)
2. Place the first 5 ingredients — cashews, eggs, olive oil, sea salt and stevia — into a high-powered blender and blend on medium-high speed until the cashews are smooth, about 50 seconds. (A traditional blender will work too; even if the cashews don't get as smooth, the recipe will turn out well.)
3. In a separate bowl, sift together the two kinds of seeds and baking soda.
4. Start the motor running on the blender again and quickly add in all of the dry ingredients. Blend for about 10 seconds, being careful not to over-mix, just until the dry ingredients are evenly incorporated. (Some blenders may not be able to handle this step, in which case, pour the wet ingredients into a medium-size mixing bowl; add the dry ingredients, folding them in briefly but thoroughly.)
5. Fold in the frozen berries and cashews with a deft, quick hand, being careful not to over-mix the batter.
6. Allow the batter to set up for 10 minutes.
7. Scoop mounded scuffin batter onto prepared baking sheets, preferably using a 3- or 4-ounce ice cream scoop with an automatic release mechanism.

8. Bake 25 to 30 minutes, until the scuffins are puffed in the center, golden brown on top, and light brown around the edges. A toothpick or sharp knife inserted into the center should come out clean, with no wet batter adhering.

9. Cool 10 minutes on the baking sheets before removing the scuffins to baking racks or serving.

loaves & muffins

CHAPTER THREE

Loaves and Muffins

Loaves and muffins are the basics of bread for which we yearn. They are the glory of what's comfortable. They round out any meal or create a meal in and of themselves. These high-protein recipes can function in either capacity: A savory, meat-filled muffin is lunch, or a loaf slice goes beautifully with homemade soup. You can even make yourself a sandwich again, without the bread being an apology.

Zucchini Bread

(stevia-sweetened)

This recipe fits into the category I call tea bread. It is a loaf, not too sweet, and equally good with butter and cheese as it is with compote, custard or by itself. It's high in protein and good fat, and it can be sliced thinly or thickly. It's great for lunch or an afternoon snack.

2 cups cashews or walnuts, soaked and still wet (see Appendix 2: Methods)

1 cup zucchini, chopped in small chunks

4 eggs, preferably grass-fed

4 egg whites, preferably grass-fed

1 tablespoon vanilla

1 teaspoon cinnamon

1/2 teaspoon cloves

heaping 1/4 teaspoon to 1/2 teaspoon powdered stevia (or 25 to 30 drops liquid stevia — NuNaturals brand preferred)

1/4 teaspoon sea salt

1/3 cup chia seeds

1/3 cup flaxseed meal

1/3 cup coconut flour

1/2 teaspoon baking soda

2/3 cup coconut oil, hard from being chilled in the refrigerator, chopped into small pieces

Yields 1 loaf.

Preheat oven to 325 degrees Fahrenheit.

1. Lightly grease a loaf pan and set it aside. (Or, if you wish to easily unmold the whole finished loaf for easier slicing and an attractive presentation, line a loaf pan with parchment, even the ends, and grease the lining.)
2. Place the first group of ingredients in the blender together: zucchini, cashews, eggs, egg whites, cinnamon, cloves, stevia, sea salt and vanilla.
3. Blend on medium speed for a full cycle, about 50 seconds, until the puree is mostly smooth.
4. Transfer the wet ingredients to the work bowl of a food processor.
5. Sift the dry ingredients into the food processor work bowl.
6. Add the hard coconut oil.
7. Process the food processor for 5 seconds first. Then pulse it on and off until all the ingredients are just mixed thoroughly, without over-mixing.
8. Pour the batter into the prepared loaf pan and bake until a sharp knife or long skewer comes out clean, at least 1 hour. Turn the heat down to 300 degrees if the outside is dark and the middle isn't yet cooked through. Check every 5 minutes for doneness after 1 hour.
9. Remove from the oven and allow it to cool before slicing.

Variations:

- If you don't have a food processor, simply omit the *cold* coconut oil that is added toward the end of the mixing process. Instead substitute 2/3 cup melted coconut oil or olive oil, adding it into the blender with the initial ingredients. The texture of the bread will be slightly different but still good.
- Add chocolate chips and walnuts to the batter, or sprinkle them on top before baking.

This is me surveying the damage: my pretty paper bundt pans burst open during baking! Accidents are bound to happen, and these little cakes still tasted great! They are topped with chocolate chips and sprouted walnuts.

Loaves and Muffins · 43

Blueberry Tea Bread

(nut-free)

In addition to its place at afternoon tea, this loaf is great served for breakfast. For those who can't have nuts due to allergies or don't have time to soak nuts, this recipe is made only with easily digestible seeds (and coconut flour) that do not need to be soaked before using.

5 eggs, preferably grass-fed

1/2 cup extra-virgin olive oil

1/4 cup coconut flour

1/4 cup chia seeds, processed into a meal in a high-powered blender or coffee grinder

1/4 cup maple syrup, local raw honey, coconut sugar, or hardwood-derived xylitol (Global Sweet brand recommended)

1 tablespoon lemon juice

1/8 teaspoon powdered stevia (or 15 to 20 drops liquid stevia — NuNaturals brand recommended)

1/4 teaspoon sea salt

1/8 cup coconut flour, in addition to the coconut flour above

1/2 teaspoon baking soda

1-1/2 to 2 cups frozen blueberries

Serves 8 to10, depending on thickness of slices.

Yields 1 loaf.

Preheat oven to 325 degrees Fahrenheit.

1. Prepare a loaf pan by lining it with parchment paper and greasing the paper with preferred fat.
2. Place the first 8 ingredients into the blender: eggs, olive oil, flour, seed meal, sweetener, lemon juice, stevia and sea salt.
3. Blend on medium speed until the batter is smooth, about 50 seconds.
4. In a small bowl, sift together the coconut flour and baking soda.
5. Start the motor of the blender and add the dry ingredients through the small opening in the lid. Process only long enough to evenly incorporate the baking soda without over-mixing, about 10 to 15 seconds.
6. Fold in the berries by hand, using a wooden or rubber spatula.
7. Pour the batter into the prepared loaf pan and bake for 45 to 60 minutes, until it is well puffed, golden brown, crispy at the edges, and a knife inserted in the center comes out clean or with a few dry crumbs adhering.
8. Remove the loaf from the oven and allow it to cool.
9. To slice the cooled bread, pull up on both sides of the parchment paper, removing it from the loaf pan.

Chocolate Berry Soufflé Muffins

(stevia-sweetened, baking soda-free, nut-free, seed-free, coconut flour-free)

These eggy morsels of yummy-goodness are soft soufflé muffins. They are made without nuts, seeds or coconut flour. There is a teeny bit of optional xanthan gum to help support their structure, which you'll want to source as nongenetically modified. But omit this ingredient if you prefer. These muffins are part popover, part soufflé and will have you licking your fingers with pleasure. As a bonus, they are sweetened only with berries and stevia.

8 eggs, preferably grass-fed

3/4 cup coconut oil, ghee or rendered animal fat, melted and cooled

1/2 cup cocoa

1/2 cup blueberries or raspberries

1/8 teaspoon powdered stevia (or 15 to 20 drops liquid stevia — NuNaturals brand preferred)

1/4 teaspoon sea salt

1/4 teaspoon xanthan gum (optional)

1 tablespoon fat in each cup

2 to 3 tablespoons mixed berries in each cup (a small handful)

Yields 6 extra-large soufflé muffins.

Preheat oven to 400 degrees Fahrenheit.

1. Prepare 6 extra-large muffin cups by adding 1 tablespoon fat to the bottom of each: coconut oil, ghee or rendered animal fat.
2. Place the muffin pan in the preheating oven to allow the fat to melt and the pan to heat.
3. Place the first 6 ingredients into a blender: eggs, cooled fat, cocoa, blueberries, sea salt and stevia.
4. Puree until smooth, about 35 to 40 seconds.
5. Turn the motor of the blender on again and sprinkle the xanthan gum in through the opening in the lid. Process briefly for 5 to 10 seconds more, until it is evenly incorporated, and then stop the motor. Do not over-process.
6. Remove the hot muffin pan from the oven and quickly, while the pan and the fat are still hot, fill each muffin cup 2/3 full with batter. Top each batter with the small handful of berries.
7. Bake the muffins on high heat until they are very puffed and browned, dark around the sides and edges, without being burned, about 15 minutes. Insert a knife into the center of one without piercing a berry to see if the inside is dry, no wet batter remaining.
8. Share the visual fun of the puffed beauties immediately with your eaters, as the soufflés will wilt.
9. Serve the muffins.

Savory Meat and Veggie Muffins, a k a Sausage and Egg Muffins

(nut-free, baking soda-free)

Intentionally GAPS-friendly, these muffins are an easy meal in your hand. Accompanied by a mug or Thermos of bone broth, they make the diet easier when you need to be away from home. Make a bundle of them and keep them in the freezer, easy to grab on the go. They also are free of baking soda, an added GAPS bonus, for a healing and satisfying food.

1 cup soaked pine nuts, wet, or sunflower seeds (or a nut of choice, if tolerated)

1 cup zucchini or carrots, grated

1 cup cooked ground beef or other ground meat (ideally cooked up with a little sea salt, 1/2 teaspoon per 1 pound meat)

6 eggs, preferably grass-fed

1/2 cup olive oil, coconut oil, ghee or rendered animal fat, melted and cooled

1/3 cup coconut flour or chia seeds

1 teaspoon oregano

1/2 teaspoon sea salt

1/8 teaspoon powdered stevia (or 10 to 15 drops liquid stevia — NuNaturals brand preferred)

Yields 6 extra-large or 12 medium-size muffins.

Preheat oven to 325 degrees Fahrenheit.

1. Prepare 6 extra-large muffin cups or 12 medium-size muffin cups by lining them with cut squares of parchment paper and spraying the paper with coconut oil, or wiping the inside of the paper with preferred grease. (Or use good-quality muffin cup liners that won't stick.)
2. Place the pine nuts, eggs, oil, coconut flour, oregano, sea salt and stevia into the blender.
3. Puree the ingredients until they are smooth, about 30 to 45 seconds.
4. Fold in zucchini and meat.
5. Pour the muffin batter into the prepared tin and bake until they are puffed, golden and a knife inserted into the center of one comes out clean — about 25 minutes.

Variations:

- Substitute grated apple and bulk pork for the zucchini and beef. Substitute 1/4 teaspoon allspice and 1/2 teaspoon sage for the oregano.
- Substitute any favorite leftover veggie for the zucchini: red bell pepper, small broccoli pieces, sautéed onions.
- Use ground turkey in place of the beef, and substitute thyme or tarragon for the oregano.
- Add 1/2 cup aged, grated cheese — or feta, if tolerated.

Sloppy Joe Muffins

(nut-free)

It goes without saying that these muffins make an easy, great and satisfying meal. They can be eaten out of hand, with a fork and knife, served with a salad on the side, or broken apart in chunks. The meat filling is surrounded by a seed-studded bread dough that is healthy and filling. I personally love the strategy involved with eating this savory treat out of hand: Each bite has a different amount of the meat filling. It's not even a jelly doughnut, and I'm excited! What is it about filled baked goods?

Dough

6 eggs, preferably grass-fed

3/4 cup extra-virgin olive oil or rendered lard, melted and cooled

1/2 cup chia seeds

1/2 cup flaxseed meal

1/4 teaspoon sea salt

scant 1/8 teaspoon powdered stevia (or 8 to 10 drops liquid stevia — NuNaturals brand preferred)

1/2 teaspoon baking soda

Yields 6 extra-large or 12 medium-size muffins.

Preheat oven to 325 degrees Fahrenheit.

1. Prepare 6 extra-large muffin cups or 12 medium-size muffin cups by lining them with cut squares of parchment paper and spraying the paper with coconut oil, or wiping the inside of the paper with preferred grease. (Or use good-quality muffin cup liners that won't stick.)
2. Place the first 6 ingredients into a blender: eggs, oil, seeds, sea salt and stevia.
3. Puree until smooth, about 50 seconds.
4. Turn the motor of the blender on again and sprinkle the baking soda in through the opening in the lid. Process briefly for 5 to 10 seconds more, until it is totally incorporated, and then stop the motor. Do not over-process.
5. Fill each muffin cup 1/3 full with batter.
6. Top each scant amount of batter with 1 to 2 frozen or partially frozen meat cubes, depending on size of muffin cups.
7. Top the meat cubes with more batter, allowing it to fall around and down the sides of the meat.
8. Bake the muffins until they are very puffed and browned, about 25 to 30 minutes for larger muffins and 20 minutes for smaller ones.
9. Serve the muffins, or allow them to cool first.

Filling

1 pound ground beef (or preferred ground meat of choice) broken up in a skillet with a spatula and cooked with 1/2 teaspoon sea salt

1 onion, diced and sautéed with 1/4 teaspoon sea salt

1 tablespoon tomato paste, organic and BPA-free

1 teaspoon chia seeds

1 teaspoon oregano

1. Mix all the filling ingredients together in a medium-size bowl, or the frying pan you used for the meat and onion.
2. Fill ice cube tray compartments with slightly bulging amounts of the meat mixture, 12 total. Reserve any remaining meat for another use.
3. Freeze the meat in the ice cube tray for a minimum of 1 hour.

Traditional Versatile Muffins

(stevia-sweetened, nut-free option)

The nut or seed you choose will affect the outcome of the muffin. Brazil nuts, for instance, make a great muffin but have a very distinctive texture and flavor that may not be pleasing to all eaters — a bit nubby and chewy, like dried coconut. Adding blueberries simply transforms it into a classic blueberry muffin, highly recommended! Pine nuts, macadamia nuts, cashews and walnuts will produce the most predictable and uniformly pleasing flavors and textures. But have fun and be creative! This recipe should become a staple for its versatility and reliability.

2 cups nut of choice, soaked and wet (see Appendix 2: Methods)

6 eggs, preferably grass-fed

3/4 cup olive oil, coconut oil, ghee or rendered animal fat, melted and cooled

1/4 teaspoon sea salt

1/8 to 1/4 teaspoon powdered stevia (or 15 to 20 drops liquid stevia — NuNaturals brand preferred)

1/4 cup your choice: coconut flour or chia seed meal (see Appendix 1: Glossary of Ingredients)

1/4 cup flaxseed meal

1/2 teaspoon baking soda

1-1/2 cups berries or diced apple

Yields 6 extra-large or 12 medium-size muffins.

Preheat oven to 325 degrees Fahrenheit.

1. Prepare 6 extra-large muffin cups or 12 medium-size muffin cups by lining them with cut squares of parchment paper and spraying the paper with coconut oil, or wiping the inside of the paper with preferred grease.
2. Place the first 5 ingredients into a blender: nuts/seeds, eggs, oil, sea salt and stevia.
3. Puree until smooth, about 50 seconds.
4. In a small bowl, sift together dry ingredients.
5. Turn the motor of the blender on again, on low speed, and sprinkle the dry ingredients in through the opening in the lid. Process briefly for 5 to 10 seconds more, until it is totally incorporated, and then stop the motor. Do not over-process.
6. Fold in the berries or diced apples.
7. Fill each muffin cup 2/3 full with batter.
8. Bake the muffins until they are very puffed and golden brown, about 25 to 30 minutes for larger muffins and 20 minutes for smaller ones. Insert a knife into the center of one without piercing a berry, to see if the inside is dry, no wet batter remaining.
9. Serve the muffins or allow them to cool first. They also freeze well.

Variations:

- Add 1/4 to 1/2 cup sweetener of choice if you want the muffins sweeter and can tolerate sweeteners other than stevia. With this variation, you may need to turn your oven temperature down to 300 degrees, as honey especially will cause the batter to brown more quickly.

Chocolate-Fig-Walnut Muffins

So many of my favorite things in one place …

2 cups walnuts, soaked and wet (see Appendix 2: Methods)

6 eggs, preferably grass-fed

1/2 cup olive oil, coconut oil, ghee or rendered animal fat, melted and cooled

1/2 cup local honey, maple syrup or hardwood-derived xylitol (Global Sweet brand recommended)

1/2 cup cocoa

1/4 cup dried figs, chopped into small pieces

1/4 cup tahini or hulled sesame seed butter

1/4 teaspoon sea salt

1/8 teaspoon powdered stevia (or 15 to 20 drops liquid stevia — NuNaturals brand preferred)

1/4 cup coconut flour

1/2 teaspoon baking soda

1/2 cup dried figs, chopped into small pieces

1/2 cup walnuts, sprouted, dehydrated and chopped

Yields 6 extra-large or 12 medium-size muffins.

Preheat oven to 325 degrees Fahrenheit.

1. Prepare 6 extra-large muffin cups or 12 medium-size muffin cups by lining them with cut squares of parchment paper and spraying the paper with coconut oil, or wiping the inside of the paper with preferred grease.

2. Place the first 9 ingredients into a high-powered blender: nuts, eggs, oil, sweetener, cocoa, figs, tahini, sea salt and stevia.

3. Puree until smooth, about 50 seconds, being aware that the dried fig pieces will be harder for the blender to process and may cause quite a ruckus.*

4. In a small bowl, sift together the dry ingredients.

5. Turn the motor of the blender on again, on low speed, and sprinkle the dry ingredients in through the opening in the lid. Process briefly for 5 to 10 seconds more, until it is totally incorporated, and then stop the motor. Do not over-process.

6. Fold in the additional dried figs and walnut pieces.

7. Fill each muffin cup 2/3 full with batter.

8. Bake the muffins until they are very puffed and golden brown, about 25 to 30 minutes for larger muffins and 20 minutes for smaller ones. Insert a knife into the center of one to see if the inside is dry, no wet batter remaining.

9. Serve the muffins or allow them to cool first. They also freeze well.

Variation:

- For Chocolate Raspberry Muffins, omit the sesame tahini and the figs; fold in 1-1/2 cups frozen raspberries at the end, just after incorporating the baking soda.

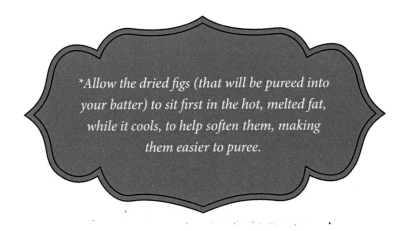

Allow the dried figs (that will be pureed into your batter) to sit first in the hot, melted fat, while it cools, to help soften them, making them easier to puree.

Apple Cinnamon Breakfast Muffins

These muffins are made with a more traditional gluten-free baking technique. Homemade sprouted nut flour and sprouted nut butter easily replace store-bought.

1-1/2 cups almond flour/meal, measured from 2-1/2 cups blended sprouted almonds

1/2 cup flaxseed meal

2 tablespoons coconut flour

1/2 teaspoon sea salt

1/2 teaspoon cinnamon

1/2 teaspoon baking soda

1/8 teaspoon powdered stevia (or 10 to 15 drops liquid stevia — NuNaturals brand preferred)

1/2 cup coconut oil

1/2 cup homemade almond butter (see Appendix 2: Methods)

1/2 cup finely chopped fresh apple or applesauce

1/3 cup packed dates

3 eggs, preferably grass-fed

1/2 cup finely chopped fresh apple or applesauce

1/2 cup walnuts (optional)

Yields 6 extra-large or 12 medium-size muffins.

Preheat oven to 325 degrees Fahrenheit.

1. Prepare 6 extra-large muffin cups or 12 medium-size muffin cups by lining them with cut squares of parchment paper and spraying the paper with coconut oil, or wiping the inside of the paper with preferred grease.
2. In a medium-size bowl, assemble and whisk together the dry ingredients: almond meal, flax, coconut flour, sea salt, cinnamon, baking soda and stevia.
3. Assemble and blend together, in a large bowl or food processor, the wet ingredients: dates, coconut oil, nut butter, apples and eggs.
4. Add the dry ingredients to the wet ingredients and mix thoroughly.
5. Fold in the apples and walnuts.
6. Drop batter into the lined muffin pan.
7. Bake until muffins are puffed, browned on top, and toothpick inserted in the center of one comes out clean.

Variations:

- For Chocolate-Peanut Butter-Banana Muffins, use peanut butter in place of the almond butter, use banana in place of the apples, one portion mashed, and one portion diced and folded in, and add 1/2 cup chocolate chips or nibs.
- For Pumpkin-Chocolate Chip Muffins, replace the pureed fresh apple with 1/2 cup cooked, mashed pumpkin, fold in 1/2 cup chocolate chips or nibs.
- If allergic to almonds, use any other sprouted nut you can tolerate to create homemade "flour" and butter; for instance, cashew flour and cashew butter would replace the almond flour and almond butter.

CHAPTER FOUR

Bars and Cookies

Nothing says family like standing in the kitchen and talking while eating freshly baked cookies. From grabbing one on the go to eating four in a row, cookies make us feel at home.

Chocolate Chip Cookies

One teeny claim to fame in this cookbook is the pioneering use of chocolate chip alternatives in chocolate chip cookies. It sounds odd, but most Paleo chocolate chip cookies still use conventional chocolate chips — a true compromise. If you can get your hands on Lily's stevia-sweetened chocolate chips, they are a good option. Otherwise, I like using shaved, organic, unsweetened chocolate! It's bitter, but the cookie dough around it is sweet. And I don't like all the fake chocolate chips on the market that substitute strange ingredients for sugar. So I say, if you can tolerate organic sugar, use the best fair-trade chocolate chips; if not, use this method or Lily's. For those who like extra work in the kitchen, consider making homemade chocolate chips,* a true labor of love. By the way, this recipe not only makes a great classic chocolate chip cookie, its soft bite allows the cookies to stay pleasantly tender in the freezer — so they make an excellent set of "heels" for ice cream sandwiches!

2 cups cashews, soaked and wet (see Appendix 2: Methods)

1/2 cup raw honey or sweetener of choice

1/2 cup coconut oil, ghee or grass-fed butter, soft or melted

2 eggs, preferably grass-fed

1/4 cup dates (optional)

1/4 cup flaxseed meal

1/4 cup chia seeds, powdered in a high-powered blender

2 teaspoons vanilla

1/4 teaspoon sea salt

1/2 teaspoon baking soda

1 cup preferred chocolate chips (or 2 ounces unsweetened chocolate, shaved or grated)

Shaving unsweetened chocolate is a great technique for quick and easy sugar-free chocolate chips.

Yields 20 cookies.

Preheat oven to 350 degrees Fahrenheit.

1. Lightly grease 2 baking sheets, or line them with parchment paper, and set aside. (Coconut oil spray can be a good tool for this step.)
2. Place cashews, honey, coconut oil, eggs, dates, vanilla and sea salt into a blender jar. Puree on medium-high speed until the cashews are smooth, about 50 seconds.
3. Transfer this wet mixture to a medium-size mixing bowl. Set aside.
4. In a small bowl, sift together seed meals and baking soda.
5. Add dry ingredients to the cashew mixture.

6. Use a hand-held or free-standing mixer (or deftly mix with a wooden spoon or spatula) to combine the ingredients thoroughly but without over-mixing. Use a spatula to scrape the cashew puree up from the bottom, making sure the bottom puree and the sides are incorporated into the body of the batter.

7. Allow the batter to "set up" for 10 minutes.

8. Scoop mounded cookie batter onto prepared cookie sheets — preferably using a 1- or 2-ounce ice cream scoop with an automatic release mechanism, or a heaping tablespoon — about 1 inch apart. (Optionally, flatten and shape them with a greased off-set spatula, if you want them to be big, flat, half-inch-thick cookies. This is how we serve them in our café. In warmer weather or with the smaller cookie size, this may not be necessary.)

9. Bake 10 to 15 minutes, until the cookies are puffed in the center, golden on top and light brown around the edges. Cool 10 minutes on the baking sheets before removing the cookies to baking racks or cut-open paper bags to cool completely.

Variations:

- Substitute 1/3 cup sweetener for 1/2 cup sweetener.
- Substitute 1/2 cup coconut flour for the flaxseed and chia seeds.

*Use slightly chilled Chocolate Ganache Frosting (Page 119) in a pastry bag to pipe small chocolate "buttons." Pipe the buttons onto a parchment lined cookie sheet. Freeze them until you are ready to use them. Peel them from the parchment. Fold them, fully chilled, into your favorite batter and proceed with the recipe. *Voila!* Homemade chocolate chips!

Chocolate Chip Cookies

(vegan, egg-free)

1 cup cashews, soaked and wet (see Appendix 2: Methods)

1 cup white beans, rinsed and preferably soaked and slow-cooked (see Appendix 2: Methods)

1/2 cup maple syrup

1/2 cup coconut oil, melted and cooled

1/2 cup flaxseed meal

1/4 cup dates

1/4 cup chia seeds

2 teaspoons vanilla

1/4 teaspoon sea salt

1/8 teaspoon vitamin C powder

1/4 cup coconut flour

1/2 teaspoon baking soda, sifted

1 cup preferred chocolate chips (or 2 ounces unsweetened chocolate, shaved or grated)

Yields 20 cookies.

Preheat oven to 325 degrees Fahrenheit.

1. Lightly grease 2 baking sheets, or line them with parchment paper, and set aside. (Coconut oil spray can be a good tool for this step.)

2. In a small bowl, sift together the coconut flour and baking soda. Set aside.

3. Place nuts, beans, maple syrup, coconut oil, flaxseed, dates, chia seeds, vanilla, sea salt and vitamin C powder into a blender jar. Puree on medium-high speed until the cashews are mostly smooth, about 35 seconds. Do not stop the motor.

4. With the motor still running, add the coconut flour and baking soda mixture, and continue pureeing for 10 more seconds.

5. Fold in the chocolate chips.

6. Allow the batter to set up for 10 minutes.

7. Scoop mounded cookie batter onto prepared cookie sheets — preferably using a 1- or 2-ounce ice cream scoop with an automatic release mechanism, or a heaping tablespoon — about 1 inch apart.

8. Bake 20 to 25 minutes, until the cookies are puffed in the center, golden on top and light brown around the edges. Cool 25 minutes on the baking sheets before removing the cookies to baking racks or cut-open paper bags to cool completely.

Chocolate Chip Cookies

(nut-free)

1 cup raw hemp seeds—or pumpkin seeds, soaked, sprouted, dehydrated and powdered into flour

1/2 cup coconut oil

1/3 cup honey, maple syrup, coconut sugar or hardwood-derived xylitol (Global Sweet brand recommended)

1/4 cup dates, broken or cut into smaller pieces

2 eggs, preferably grass-fed

1 tablespoon chia seeds, powdered

2 teaspoons vanilla

1/4 teaspoon sea salt

1/8 teaspoon stevia

1/4 cup coconut flour

1/2 teaspoon baking soda

Yields 12 cookies.

Preheat oven to 350 degrees Fahrenheit.

1. Lightly grease 2 baking sheets, or line them with parchment paper, and set aside. (Coconut oil spray can be a good tool for this step.)
2. Place hemp or pumpkin seeds, coconut oil, sweetener, dates, eggs, chia seeds, vanilla, sea salt and stevia into a blender jar. Puree on medium-high speed until the batter is smooth, about 50 seconds.

3. Transfer this wet mixture to a medium-size mixing bowl. Set aside.

4. In a small bowl, sift together the flour and baking soda.

5. Add dry ingredients to the batter mixture.

6. Use a hand-held or free-standing mixer (or deftly mix with a wooden spoon or spatula) to combine the ingredients thoroughly but without over-mixing. Use a spatula to scrape the batter puree up from the bottom, making sure the bottom puree and the sides are incorporated into the body of the batter.

7. Allow the batter to set up for 10 minutes.

8. Scoop mounded cookie batter onto prepared cookie sheets — preferably using a 1- or 2-ounce ice cream scoop with an automatic release mechanism, or a heaping tablespoon — about 1 inch apart.

9. Bake 10 to 15 minutes, until the cookies are puffed in the center, golden on top and light brown around the edges. Cool 10 minutes on the baking sheets before removing the cookies to baking racks or cut-open paper bags to cool completely.

Bacon-Chocolate Chip-Walnut Cookies

These are granola-meets-Paleo, meat-meets-nutmeat treats. I love them — healthy-tasting and indulgent all at once.

1-1/2 cups walnuts, soaked, sprouted and dehydrated

1/4 cup rendered bacon fat

1/4 cup coconut oil

1/3 cup honey, maple syrup, coconut sugar or hardwood-derived xylitol (Global Sweet brand recommended)

1/4 cup dates (optional)

2 eggs, preferably grass-fed

1 teaspoon vanilla

1/4 teaspoon sea salt

1/4 cup flaxseed meal

1/8 cup coconut flour

1/2 teaspoon baking soda

1/2 cup bacon, chopped

1/2 cup preferred chocolate chips (or 1 ounce unsweetened chocolate, minced, grated or shaved)

1/2 cup walnuts, soaked, sprouted and dehydrated

Yields 20 cookies.

Preheat oven to 350 degrees Fahrenheit.

1. Lightly grease 2 baking sheets, or line them with parchment paper, and set aside. (Coconut oil spray can be a good tool for this step.)

2. Place walnuts, sweetener, bacon fat, coconut oil, eggs, dates, vanilla and sea salt into a blender jar. Puree on medium-high speed until the walnuts are smooth, about 50 seconds.

3. Transfer this wet mixture to a medium-size mixing bowl. Set aside.

4. In a small bowl, sift together flaxseed meal, flour and baking soda.

5. Add dry ingredients, bacon, chocolate chips and walnuts to the nut batter mixture.

6. Use a hand-held or free-standing mixer (or deftly mix with a wooden spoon or spatula) to combine the ingredients thoroughly but without over-mixing. Use a spatula to scrape the batter puree up from the bottom, making sure the bottom puree and the sides are incorporated into the body of the batter.

7. Allow the batter to "set up" for 10 minutes.

8. Scoop mounded cookie batter onto prepared cookie sheets — preferably using a 1- or 2-ounce ice cream scoop with an automatic release mechanism, or a heaping tablespoon — about 1 inch apart.

9. Bake 10 to 15 minutes, until the cookies are puffed in the center, golden on top and light brown around the edges. Cool 10 minutes on the baking sheets before removing the cookies to baking racks or cut-open paper bags to cool completely.

Halvah Cookies

(nut-free)

This is a recipe my mom loves. I dedicate it to her, in fond memory of several Jewish foods we enjoyed while growing up.

4 eggs, preferably grass-fed

1/4 cup coconut flour

1/4 cup tahini, or hulled sesame seed butter

1/4 cup chia seeds, powdered in a high-powered blender

1/4 cup coconut oil

1/4 cup honey

2 tablespoons cocoa powder

1 teaspoon vanilla

1 teaspoon cinnamon

1/4 teaspoon sea salt

1/8 teaspoon stevia

1/4 cup flaxseed meal

1/2 teaspoon baking soda

Yields 12 cookies.

Preheat oven to 350 degrees Fahrenheit.

1. Lightly grease 2 baking sheets, or line them with parchment paper, and set aside. (Coconut oil spray can be a good tool for this step.)
2. Place the first group of ingredients into a blender jar: eggs, flour, tahini, powdered chia seeds, coconut oil, honey, cocoa powder, vanilla, cinnamon, sea salt and stevia. Puree on medium-high speed until the batter is smooth, about 25 seconds.
3. Transfer this wet mixture to a medium-size mixing bowl. Set aside.
4. In a small bowl, sift together the flour and baking soda.
5. Add the dry ingredients to the nut batter mixture.
6. Use a hand-held or free-standing mixer (or deftly mix with a wooden spoon or spatula) to combine the ingredients thoroughly but without over-mixing. Use a spatula to scrape the batter puree up from the bottom, making sure the bottom puree and the sides are incorporated into the body of the batter.
7. Allow the batter to "set up" for 10 minutes.
8. Scoop mounded cookie batter onto prepared cookie sheets — preferably using a 1- or 2-ounce ice cream scoop with an automatic release mechanism, or a heaping tablespoon — about 1 inch apart.
9. Bake 10 to 15 minutes, until the cookies are puffed in the center, golden on top and light brown around the edges. Cool 10 minutes on the baking sheets before removing the cookies to baking racks or cut-open paper bags, to cool completely.

These three cookie batters bake into cookie "bobbles" unless they are spread out with a greased spatula to be flatter rounds. We actually like the moistness in these recipes when the cookies are kept rounded before baking.

Although the platter of chocolatey-looking cookies appears to be one variety, it is actually three, from left to right: Halvah, Pumpkin, and Cinnamon Snickerdoodle. All get rave reviews from my mom and husband, the in-the-closet and self-professed cookie lovers in my life!

Breakfast Porridge Apple Cookies

(nut-free)

My hubby loves these. They taste like applesauce-chia porridge in cookie form — humble, healthy and a good breakfast on the go.

1/2 cup coconut oil

1/3 cup sweetener of choice: local raw honey, maple syrup, coconut sugar or hardwood-derived xylitol (Global Sweet brand recommended)

1/2 large Granny Smith apple, cored but not peeled

2 eggs, preferably grass-fed

1/3 cup chia seeds, powdered in a high-powered blender

2 teaspoons vanilla

1/2 teaspoon cinnamon

1/4 teaspoon sea salt

1/4 teaspoon allspice

1/2 cup coconut flour

1/2 teaspoon baking soda

Yields 12 cookies.

Preheat oven to 350 degrees Fahrenheit.

1. Lightly grease 2 baking sheets, or line them with parchment paper, and set aside. (Coconut oil spray can be a good tool for this step.)

2. Place the first 9 ingredients into a blender jar: coconut oil, sweetener, apple, eggs, seeds, vanilla, cinnamon, allspice and sea salt. Puree on medium-high speed until the batter is smooth, about 25 seconds.

3. Transfer this wet mixture to a medium-size mixing bowl. Set aside.

4. In a small bowl, sift together the flour and baking soda.

5. Add dry ingredients to the seed batter mixture.

6. Use a hand-held or free-standing mixer (or deftly mix with a wooden spoon or spatula) to combine the ingredients thoroughly, but without over-mixing. Use a spatula to scrape the batter puree up from the bottom, making sure the bottom puree and the sides are incorporated into the body of the batter.

7. Allow the batter to "set up" for 10 minutes.

8. Scoop mounded cookie batter onto prepared cookie sheets — preferably using a 2- to 3-ounce ice cream scoop with an automatic release mechanism, or 2 heaping tablespoons — about 1 inch apart.

9. Bake 12 to 15 minutes, until the cookies are puffed in the center, golden on top and light brown around the edges. Cool 10 minutes on the baking sheets before removing the cookies to baking racks or cut-open paper bags to cool completely.

Classic Pumpkin Spice Cookies

1-1/2 cups wet, soaked cashews or walnuts (see Appendix 2: Methods)

1 cup organic cooked pumpkin, or BPA-free canned pumpkin

1/2 cup coconut oil, melted and cooled

3 eggs, preferably grass-fed

1/4 cup raw honey or sweetener of choice

1/4 cup flaxseed meal (or substitute coconut flour)

1/4 cup chia seeds, powdered (or substitute coconut flour)

1 tablespoon minced fresh ginger (or 1 teaspoon dried ginger)

1 teaspoon cinnamon

1/2 teaspoon baking soda

1/2 teaspoon each: allspice, nutmeg, cloves

1/4 teaspoon sea salt

1/8 teaspoon powdered stevia (or 15 to 20 drops liquid stevia — NuNaturals brand preferred)

Yields 20 cookies.

Preheat oven to 350 degrees Fahrenheit.

1. Lightly grease 2 baking sheets, or line them with parchment paper, and set aside. (Coconut oil spray can be a good tool for this step.)
2. Place nuts, coconut oil, pumpkin and eggs into a blender jar. Puree on medium-high speed until the cashews are smooth, about 50 seconds.
3. Transfer this wet mixture to a medium-size mixing bowl. Set aside.

4. In a medium-size bowl, sift together seed meals (or coconut flour), baking soda, sea salt, spices and stevia.

5. Add raw honey and dry ingredients to the mixing bowl. Add fresh ginger, if using.

6. Use a hand-held or free-standing mixer (or deftly mix with a wooden spoon) to whisk together the ingredients thoroughly but without over-mixing. Use a spatula to scrape up from the bottom the nut puree, making sure the bottom and sides are incorporated into the body of the batter.

7. Allow the batter to "set up" for 10 minutes.

8. Scoop mounded cookie batter onto prepared cookie sheets — preferably using a 1- or 2-ounce ice cream scoop with an automatic release mechanism, or a heaping tablespoon — about 1 inch apart.

9. Bake 10 to 15 minutes, until the cookies are puffed in the center, golden on top and light brown around the edges. Cool 10 minutes on the baking sheets before removing the cookies to baking racks or cut-open paper bags to cool completely.

Variations:

- These cookies can be topped with Hazelnut Buttercream frosting (Page 133).
- Substitute 1/2 cup coconut flour for the flaxseed and chia seed meals.

"Oatmeal-Raisin" Cookies

Yep, no grains about it, these cookies even smell like the classic. Enjoy a new twist on an old favorite.

2 cups cashews, soaked and wet (see Appendix 2: Methods)

2 eggs, preferably grass-fed

1/3 cup coconut oil, grass-fed butter or ghee, melted and cooled

1/4 cup maple syrup, local raw honey, coconut sugar or hardwood-derived xylitol (Global Sweet brand recommended)

2 teaspoons vanilla

1/2 cup flaxseed meal

1 teaspoon cinnamon

1/2 teaspoon baking soda

1/8 teaspoon sea salt

1/8 teaspoon stevia

3/4 cup raisins

Yields 12 cookies.

Preheat oven to 325 degrees Fahrenheit.

1. Lightly grease 2 baking sheets or line them with parchment paper, and set aside. (Coconut oil spray can be a good tool for this step.)
2. Place the nuts, eggs, coconut oil, sweetener and vanilla into a blender jar. Puree on medium-high speed until the cashews are smooth, about 50 seconds.

3. Transfer this wet mixture to a medium-size mixing bowl. Set aside.
4. In a small bowl, sift together the flaxseed meal, cinnamon, baking soda, sea salt and stevia.
5. Pour the dry ingredients into the bowl with the wet ingredients.
6. Use a hand-held or free-standing mixer (or deftly mix with a wooden spoon) to combine the ingredients thoroughly but without over-mixing. Use a spatula to scrape up from the bottom the nut puree, making sure the bottom and sides are incorporated into the body of the batter.
7. Fold in the raisins.
8. Allow the batter to "set up" for 10 minutes.
9. Scoop mounded cookie batter onto prepared cookie sheets — preferably using a 1- or 2-ounce ice cream scoop with an automatic release mechanism, or a heaping tablespoon — about 1 inch apart.
10. Bake 10 to 15 minutes, until the cookies are puffed in the center, golden on top and light brown around the edges. Cool 10 minutes on the baking sheets before removing the cookies to baking racks or cut-open paper bags to cool completely.

Macadamia Nut Snickerdoodles

Well-liked by all, these cookies could be called ketogenic, meaning super-high in good fats, containing no sugar and little protein. They come out pretty dark from all the cinnamon paired with pale nuts, but they taste like a lovely version of the soft, blond snickerdoodles we've all known and loved. We like to bake them puffy, as opposed to flattening them out before baking. That way you get a more doughy middle.

1-3/4 cup raw macadamia nuts, soaked and wet (see Appendix 2: Methods)

1/2 cup unsalted butter, softened, preferably grass-fed

1/3 cup egg whites, preferably grass-fed (save the yolks to make custard or eggnog)

1/3 cup hardwood-derived xylitol (Global Sweet brand recommended)

1/3 cup flaxseed meal

1-1/2 teaspoon cinnamon

1/2 teaspoon baking soda

1/4 teaspoon heaping sea salt

Yields 12 cookies.

Preheat oven to 325 degrees Fahrenheit.

1. Lightly grease 2 baking sheets, or line them with parchment paper, and set aside. (Coconut oil spray can be a good tool for this step.)
2. Place the nuts, butter, egg whites and xylitol into a blender jar. Puree on medium-high speed until the nuts are smooth, about 50 seconds.
3. Transfer this wet mixture to a medium-size mixing bowl. Set aside.
4. In a small bowl, sift together the flaxseed meal, cinnamon, baking soda and sea salt.
5. Pour the dry ingredients into the bowl with the wet ingredients.
6. Use a hand-held or free-standing mixer, (or deftly mix with a wooden spoon) to combine the ingredients thoroughly but without over-mixing. Use a spatula to scrape up from the bottom the nut puree, making sure the bottom and sides are incorporated into the body of the batter.
7. Allow the batter to "set up" for 10 minutes.
8. Scoop mounded cookie batter onto prepared cookie sheets — preferably using a 1- or 2-ounce ice cream scoop with an automatic release mechanism, or a heaping tablespoon — about 1 inch apart.
9. Bake 10 to 15 minutes, until the cookies are puffed in the center, golden on top and light brown around the edges. Cool 10 minutes on the baking sheets before removing the cookies to baking racks or cut-open paper bags to cool completely.

Chocolate Chip Cake Bars

These are quick, healthy and so comforting you won't know whether to call them a cake or a cookie.

2 cups cashews, soaked and wet (see Appendix 2: Methods)

1/2 cup coconut oil, melted and cooled

1/3 cup raw honey or other sweetener of choice

2 eggs, preferably grass-fed

1/4 teaspoon sea salt

2 ounces shaved unsweetened chocolate, or preferred chocolate chips

1/4 cup coconut flour

1/2 teaspoon baking soda, sifted

Yields 9 to 16 bars.

Preheat oven to 325 degrees Fahrenheit.

1. Grease a 9-inch square pan with coconut oil or sustainably sourced lard.
2. In a food processor or high-powered blender, combine the first 5 ingredients: cashews, coconut oil, sweetener, eggs and sea salt.
3. Puree until smooth, stopping the motor once or twice to scrape down the sides of the mixing bowl.
4. In a separate small bowl, sift together the coconut flour and baking soda.

5. Sprinkle the sifted mixture and the shaved chocolate over the top of the wet ingredients, and process briefly but thoroughly once more, being careful not to over-mix.

6. Pour the batter into the greased pan and bake until the center is puffed, the edges are golden brown and a toothpick inserted in the center comes out clean or with tiny small crumbs adhering.

7. Allow it to cool on a drying rack before slicing into squares and removing with an offset spatula.

Variation:

- To make Pumpkin Chocolate Chip Cake Bars, my kids' favorite, add 1/2 cup cooked winter squash or canned pumpkin, 1/3 cup flaxseed meal and 1/2 teaspoon cinnamon to the wet ingredients. Decrease the coconut flour to 2 tablespoons. Proceed with the rest of the recipe as usual.

Pumpkin Pie Bars with Chocolate-Lined Crust

(stevia-sweetened option, nut-free option)

For my 40th birthday, we drove to the Pacific Coast, a renewing setting for me, and brought with us a "hamper" containing a GAPS-friendly feast. This was the dessert I chose to bring along. I could eat these until the cows come home. They have just enough bittersweet chocolate to make chocolate lovers happy and enough creamy pumpkin to make them healthy and comforting. They can be made with stevia alone for fructose-restricted diets. (Substitute a seed crust, — Page 97 — and peanut (a legume) or sunflower seed butter for the nut butter, if you are nut-free.)

Filling

3 cups cooked kabocha squash (see Appendix 2: Methods), or 1-1/2 cans BPA-free, organic, canned pumpkin

1/4 cup honey, maple syrup, coconut sugar or hardwood-derived xylitol (Global Sweet brand recommended) (optional)

1/2 cup extra-virgin coconut oil or homemade sprouted nut butter (see Appendix 2: Methods)

2 teaspoons vanilla

1 teaspoon cinnamon

1 teaspoon ginger

1/2 teaspoon each: allspice, cloves and nutmeg

1/8 teaspoon powdered stevia (or 20 drops liquid stevia — NuNaturals brand preferred)*

1 tablespoon sustainably sourced gelatin

1/2 cup water, room temperature

Bittersweet Chocolate Lining

1/4 cup cocoa powder

1/4 cup coconut oil, melted and still warm

1/16 teaspoon powdered stevia (or 8 to 10 drops liquid stevia — or 1/8 cup sweetener of choice, such as honey or maple syrup)

pinch sea salt

Crust

2 cups almonds or walnuts, sprouted and dehydrated

4 tablespoons coconut oil, melted

2 tablespoons xylitol (Global Sweet brand recommended) or coconut sugar, or 1/16 teaspoon powdered stevia (NuNaturals brand recommended)

pinch sea salt

Yields 16 bars.

Preheat oven to 375 degrees Fahrenheit.

Bake the winter squash first. See instructions below. Then prepare the crust, allowing it time to cool while you prepare the filling.

1. Place the nuts into the work bowl of a food processor.
2. Process them until the nuts are as small as you prefer. Ideally, some of them will be powdered nut meal and some small pieces will remain. Avoid processing long enough to create a nut butter.
3. Add the coconut oil, sweetener of choice and sea salt.
4. Pulse the coconut oil into the nuts until a crumble texture has formed and no large pieces of coconut oil remain.

5. Press the nut mixture into a 9-inch square pan, creating an even firm crust up the sides of the pan by 1 inch, pushing down on the top side-edges so they are smooth and neat.
6. Bake the crust for 8 to 10 minutes, until it is browned slightly and fragrant.
7. Set it aside to cool while you prepare the lining and filling. If you want to speed things up, (and your squash is already ready), put the crust in the freezer until you need it.
8. In a small bowl, whisk together all the lining ingredients until thoroughly homogenized. Set aside.
9. Place the cooked winter squash, sweetener, oil or nut butter, vanilla, spices and stevia into a food processor or blender and puree until smooth, about 20 to 30 seconds. Set aside.
10. Into a medium-size saucepan, pour the remaining 1/2 cup water. Sprinkle the surface with the gelatin. Allow the gelatin to dissolve on the surface of the water for 1 minute.
11. Turn the burner heat to medium and stir the water and gelatin.
12. After about 3 minutes, the mixture will be steaming, but not yet simmering. Turn off the heat.
13. Add the gelatin water to the winter squash mixture and puree until the two are mixed well.
14. Into the cooled or cold crust, evenly drizzle the chocolate lining, spreading it evenly over the crust with an offset spatula.
15. Put it into the refrigerator for 10 to 15 minutes to allow it to harden off, unless the crust was frozen first — in which case the lining will harden immediately.
16. Now pour the filling into the chocolate-lined crust and refrigerate for a minimum of 6 hours, or overnight.
17. Slice into approximately 2-1/2-inch square bars and enjoy.

*Add 1/16 teaspoon stevia (or to taste) if omitting the additional sweetener of choice above.

How to Cook a Kabocha Squash

Preheat oven to 375 degrees Fahrenheit.

1. Bake the squash for 1-1/2 hours, or until very tender when poked deeply with a knife.
2. Allow it to cool slightly, and then cut it in half through the middle, as if cutting a "hat" off.
3. Open the lid of the squash and scoop the seeds from the seed cavity.
4. Measure out 3 cups winter squash.

Pumpkin Cream Cheese Bars

Make these bars in an 8-inch square pan, a 9-inch square pan, or a 2-quart glass baking dish. They are a classic treat, with the cream cheese swirling into the batter and baking into a pretty top pattern that leaves creamy, rich pockets. My favorite compliment regarding these bars came from a customer who asked with incredulity and swooning pleasure, "Are these healthy? They don't taste healthy." I love baked goods that taste like an indulgent pastry but in actuality fill your body with easy-to-digest nourishment.

If you want the showy golden swirls from the cream cheese topping, it is best to chill the swirl ingredients a minimum of 3 hours or even overnight. The swirl mixture still works at room temperature, but it is runny and requires you to use a spatula to create canals in the batter to pour the swirl into. Otherwise, it will cover the surface of the batter without swirling, due to its quantity. All of these methods actually work and taste great. For the fastest, easiest method, just pour and spread the Cream Cheese Swirl mixture onto the surface of the bars. The bottom cake layer will be thick and the cream cheese layer will be like a baked frosting. But if you want the prettiest swirl, chill your Cream Cheese Swirl mixture well first, place it in a piping bag, as you would with frosting, and decorate the top of the bars accordingly. When the batter bakes, it will swell up and around the swirls to some extent.

Batter

2 cups cashews, soaked and wet (see Appendix 2: Methods)

4 eggs, preferably grass-fed

3/4 cup coconut oil, melted and cooled slightly

1/2 cup BPA-free canned pumpkin or leftover cooked winter squash, such as kabocha or butternut

1/4 cup dates, pieces cut up and then measured, packed

1/4 cup local, raw honey

1 teaspoon cinnamon

1 teaspoon ginger

1/4 teaspoon sea salt

1/8 teaspoon powdered stevia (preferably NuNuturals brand)

1/3 cup flaxseed meal

3 tablespoons coconut flour

1/2 teaspoon baking soda

Cream Cheese Swirl

1 8-ounce package organic cream cheese, at room temperature

1/4 cup local, raw honey

1 egg, preferably grass-fed

Yields 9 to 16 bars.

Preheat oven to 325 degrees Fahrenheit.

1. Grease a 9-inch square pan with coconut oil or sustainably sourced lard.
2. In a medium-size bowl, whisk or beat together the Cream Cheese Swirl ingredients thoroughly, until smooth and well-mixed. Refrigerate the swirl until you are ready to use it.
3. In a food processor or high-powered blender, combine the first group of ingredients: cashews, eggs, coconut oil, pumpkin, dates, honey, spices, sea salt and stevia.
4. Puree until smooth, stopping the motor once or twice to scrape down the sides of the mixing bowl.
5. In a separate small bowl, sift together the flaxseed meal, coconut flour and baking soda.
6. Sprinkle the sifted mixture over the top of the wet ingredients; process briefly but thoroughly once more, being careful not to over-mix.
7. Pour the batter into the prepared pan.
8. Pour the Cream Cheese Swirl ingredients over the batter in a swirling pattern, using a rubber spatula to spread the swirl in even amounts over the surface and into the batter. Or use a piping bag to swirl the topping decoratively, if you have chilled it for the longer period of time mentioned above.
9. Bake until the center is puffed, the edges and top are golden brown and a toothpick inserted in the center comes out clean or with tiny small crumbs adhering. If the top browns too quickly, cover the pan loosely with parchment paper or a lid for the last 10 minutes of baking.
10. Allow to cool on a drying rack before slicing into squares and removing with an offset spatula.

Variations:

- Use Berry Compote (Page 199) on the surface of the wet batter, adding small spoonfuls on top of and around the cream cheese swirl. The bars will be moist and decadent, delicious and beautiful to look at.

- Bake the batter in a 9-inch-by-13-inch pan for thinner bars that will bake more quickly.

Gooey Brownies

These are classic brownies, a customer favorite. The three different sweeteners each contribute to the right flavor profile (not too strong of a honey flavor, for instance) and also make a big impact on the texture I look for in a brownie: a bit cakey, a bit dense and a bit gooey.

3/4 cup cocoa powder

1/2 cup maple syrup

1/2 cup raw honey

1/2 cup coconut oil, butter or ghee

1/2 cup dates, broken into small pieces

1/4 cup hardwood-derived xylitol (Global Sweet brand recommended) or coconut sugar

4 eggs

2 teaspoons vanilla

1/2 teaspoon sea salt

1/4 cup flaxseed meal

2 tablespoons coconut flour

1/2 teaspoon baking soda

Yields 12 to 16 brownies.

Preheat oven to 325 degrees Fahrenheit.

1. Prepare a 9-inch square pan by lining it with parchment paper and greasing the paper. This will enable you to lift out the cooled brownies in one piece and slice them more easily into squares.

2. Combine in a blender or food processor the first 9 ingredients: cocoa, maple syrup, honey, xylitol or coconut sugar, fat, dates, eggs, sea salt and vanilla.

3. Blend on low speed, pulsing as necessary, for about 50 seconds.

4. In a small bowl, sift together the remaining dry ingredients.

5. Scrape down the sides of the blender or work bowl and add the remaining dry ingredients: flaxseed meal, coconut flour and baking soda.

6. Blend to evenly incorporate the dry ingredients without over-mixing. (If you used xylitol, the mixture will be grainy and not as runny; so you may need to fold in the dry ingredients by hand, if using a blender.)

7. Pour the liquid batter, (or scoop and spread the xylitol-based batter), into the prepared pan. Use a spatula to spread the batter evenly to all of the edges and corners.

8. Bake in the preheated oven for 30 to 35 minutes, until the edges are dry and only the very center (3 to 4 inches in diameter) is not yet cracked but is raised or puffed from the heat.

9. Allow the brownies to cool completely before pulling up on the paper sides, sliding a metal off-set spatula underneath all parts of the brownies to loosen the paper's seal with the pan, and lifting the brownies out to a cutting surface. Or chill the cooled brownies for 3 to 6 hours (or overnight) before slicing.

10. Cut brownies into desired size and serve.

Variations:
- Replace the maple syrup and honey with 3/4 cup hardwood-derived xylitol (Global Sweet brand recommended).
- Use the chilled cream cheese swirl from Page 86 to make Classic Cream Cheese Swirl Brownies.

pies

CHAPTER FIVE

Pies

American history is alive and well. Skip the contributions from the first half of the 20th century (when Crisco and margarine propaganda lured housewives away from butter, lard and coconut oil). I have observed pie devotees transported with happiness by a perfect wedge of their preferred dessert. Pie combines a crumbly or flaky crust with something rich and sticky. I like to use a spoon for scooping up bites of pie (a fork won't do for holding in the goo). The recipes in this chapter revolutionize your grain-free crust options. Some of the fillings blow away what we've come to see as normal, while many keep with and honor tradition. No more tapioca pearls or cornstarch. But bring on the classics. See and taste a whole new world of fork (or spoon) to mouth.

Kiwi Lime Pie

Happy Omega Pie Crust

1-1/2 cups walnuts, soaked, sprouted and dehydrated

1/2 cup hemp seeds

6 pitted dates, roughly chopped

pinch of sea salt

Yields 1 pie crust. Adapted from a recipe in Internal Bliss, *a cookbook by Dr. Natasha Campbell-McBride.*

1. Place the nuts, seeds and dates into the work bowl of a food processor.
2. Process them until the nuts are as small as you prefer. Ideally, some of them will be powdered nut meal and some small pieces will remain. The dates will begin to create sticky clumps.
3. Press this mixture into the bottom and up the sides of a pie plate.
4. Chill crust until you are ready to use it.

Variation:

- Roll this mixture into balls. Roll the balls in cocoa powder or hemp seeds. Place the balls in the freezer and use as you would granola bars for quick, high-energy snacks on the go. Add 1/2 teaspoon spirulina in Step 1 for added nutrition.

Kiwi-Lime Filling *(egg-free, dairy-free, mostly raw)*

1 cup avocado, the sliced flesh smashed slightly to measure its quantity accurately

1 whole kiwi, peeled and cut in half

1/2 cup freshly squeezed lime juice

1/2 cup sweetener of choice: honey, maple syrup, coconut sugar or 1/3 cup xylitol (Global Sweet brand recommended)

1/2 cup extra-virgin coconut oil, melted and cooled

1/4 cup organic coconut milk

2 teaspoons vanilla

1/8 teaspoon powdered stevia (or 8 to 10 drops liquid stevia — NuNaturals brand preferred)

pinch of sea salt

Yields filling for 1 pie. Adapted from a recipe in Internal Bliss, *a cookbook by Dr. Natasha Campbell-McBride.*

1. Place ingredients in a food processor or blender.
2. Process until smooth, about 30 to 40 seconds.
3. Pour filling into prepared pie crust and freeze for a minimum of 3 hours.
4. Remove 1 hour before serving for optimum texture.
5. Slice and serve. Garnish with fresh kiwi, kiwi berries or strawberries.

Mixed Berry-Avocado Pie

(dairy-free, egg-free, nut-free option)

Brazil Nut Crust

2 cups Brazil nuts or almonds, soaked, sprouted and dehydrated (or use seeds for a nut-free option)

1/4 cup room-temperature or cold coconut oil, broken into 4 or more pieces

1/4 teaspoon cloves

1/16 teaspoon powdered stevia

Yields 1 pie crust.

Preheat oven to 350 degrees Fahrenheit.

1. Prepare crust first, allowing it time to cool while you prepare the filling.
2. Place the nuts into the work bowl of a food processor.
3. Process until the nuts are as small as you prefer — ideally, some will be powdered and some small pieces will remain — but not long enough to create a nut butter.
4. Add coconut oil, cloves and stevia.
5. Pulse the coconut oil into the nuts until a crumble texture has formed and no large pieces of coconut oil remain.
6. Press nut mixture into a 9-inch pie plate, creating an even, firm crust, up the sides of the pan, too, pushing down on the top side edges so they are smooth and neat. Scallop them slightly, if desired.
7. Bake crust for 8 to 10 minutes, until it is browned slightly and fragrant.
8. Set it aside to cool while you prepare the filling.

Mixed Berry-Avocado Filling

1-3/4 cups mixed berries, defrosted if frozen (reserve 1 cup for folding in at the end)

2 small avocados, peeled and cut into quarters

1/2 cup dates, packed to measure but then broken into smaller pieces

1/2 cup lemon juice

1/2 cup water

1/4 cup extra-virgin coconut oil, melted

1 tablespoon + 1 teaspoon sustainably sourced gelatin

1/8 teaspoon powdered stevia (or 8 to 10 drops liquid stevia— NuNaturals brand preferred)

Yields filling for 1 pie.

1. Place the ½ cup water in a small saucepan. Sprinkle the gelatin over its surface. Allow it to dissolve for 1 minute.
2. Turn the heat to medium, stirring the water and gelatin. Continue stirring to fully dissolve the gelatin.
3. After about 3 minutes, the mixture will be steaming, but not yet simmering. Turn off the heat.
4. Into your blender place the following ingredients: 3/4 cup defrosted berries, avocados, melted coconut oil, date pieces, lemon juice, gelatin water and stevia.
5. Puree on medium speed for about 50 seconds, until the mixture is smooth.
6. Fold in the reserved whole berries.
7. Pour the mixture into the cooled piecrust and refrigerate for a minimum of 6 hours or overnight.
8. Serve garnished with fresh berries, whipped cream, lightly sweetened cultured cream or nothing at all.

Carrot-Cinnamon Mousse Pie

(dairy-free, egg-free, nut-free option, stevia-sweetened)

Anyone with "leaky gut" might know the importance of rotating seeds and nuts to avoid acquiring a new food allergy. Seeds are a great choice for many who are already allergic to most nuts. This recipe fits the bill. Made only with pumpkin seeds, the crust can easily be adapted (by using the delicious pine nut option). This pie is rich and indulgent. It gives your body great nutrients without any added sweeteners other than the carrots themselves and stevia.

Italian Nut or Seed Pie Crust

Umbria, in Italy, is famous for walnut-based recipes based on its abundant local walnut harvest. And, of course, all over Italy, pine nuts have earned a reputation for their rich, unique flavor. This crust is versatile and works well with either option.

2 cups walnuts or Italian pine nuts (which are actually seeds), soaked and dehydrated

1/4 cup room-temperature or cold extra-virgin coconut oil or ghee, broken into 4 or more pieces

1/16 teaspoon powdered stevia (NuNaturals brand preferred)

Yields 1 pie crust.

Preheat oven to 350 degrees Fahrenheit.

1. Prepare crust first, allowing it time to cool while you prepare the filling.
2. Place the nuts into the work bowl of a food processor.
3. Process until the nuts are as small as you prefer — ideally, some will be powdered and some small pieces will remain — but not long enough to create a nut butter.

4. Add coconut oil and stevia.

5. Pulse the coconut oil into the nuts until a crumble texture has formed and no large pieces of coconut oil remain.

6. Press nut mixture into a 9-inch pie plate, creating an even, firm crust, up the sides of the pan, too, pushing down on the top side edges so they are smooth and neat. Scallop them slightly, if desired.

7. Bake crust for 8 to 10 minutes, until it is browned slightly and fragrant.

8. Set it aside to cool while you prepare the filling.

Carrot Cinnamon Filling

2 cups steamed carrots, fork-tender

1-1/2 cups raw pumpkin seeds, soaked, rinsed and still wet

1 cup extra-virgin coconut oil, melted

1 teaspoon cinnamon

1/8 teaspoon stevia (or 1/4 cup honey or preferred sweetener of choice)

1 cup water

1 tablespoon + 1 teaspoon sustainably sourced gelatin

Yields filling for 1 pie.

1. Place 1 cup water in a small saucepan. Sprinkle gelatin over its surface. Allow it to dissolve for 1 minute.

2. Turn the heat to medium, and stir the water and gelatin. Continue stirring to mix and fully dissolve the gelatin.

3. After about 3 minutes, the mixture will be steaming but not yet simmering. Turn off the heat.

4. Place the following ingredients into a blender: cooked carrots, pumpkin seeds, coconut oil, cinnamon, stevia and the slightly cooled gelatin water.

5. Puree on medium-high speed until the ingredients are completely smooth, about 50 seconds.

6. Pour filling into the prepared, cooled crust and refrigerate for a minimum of 6 hours, or overnight.

Pumpkin Pie

(egg-free)

Plan ahead: See steps 8 through 11 below to prepare squash before making pie.

Simple Nut Crust Ingredients (stevia-sweetened)

2 cups walnuts, hazelnuts or almonds, soaked and dehydrated

1/4 cup room-temperature or cold coconut oil or ghee, broken into 4 or more pieces

1/16 teaspoon stevia

Yields 1 pie crust.

Preheat oven to 350 degrees Fahrenheit.

1. Prepare crust first, allowing it time to cool while you prepare the filling.
2. Place the nuts into the work bowl of a food processor.
3. Process until the nuts are as small as you prefer — ideally, some will be powdered and some small pieces will remain — but not long enough to create a nut butter.
4. Add coconut oil and stevia.
5. Pulse the coconut oil into the nuts until a crumble texture has formed and no large pieces of coconut oil remain.
6. Press nut mixture into a 9-inch pie plate, creating an even, firm crust, up the sides of the pan, too, pushing down on the top side edges so they are smooth and neat. Scallop them slightly, if desired.

7. Bake crust for 8 to 10 minutes, until it is browned slightly and fragrant.
8. Set it aside to cool while you prepare the filling.

Pumpkin Filling

2 cups baked kabocha squash, (see Appendix 2: Methods), or 1 can BPA-free, organic, canned pumpkin

1 cup water

1/2 cup creamy coconut milk

1/2 cup additional water, room temperature

1/4 cup extra-virgin coconut oil

1/4 cup honey or sweetener of choice

1 tablespoon sustainably sourced gelatin

1 teaspoon cinnamon

1 teaspoon ginger

1/8 teaspoon powdered stevia (optional)

Yields filling for 1 pie.

1. Bake the kabocha squash for 1-1/2 hours, or until very tender when poked deeply with a knife.
2. Allow it to cool slightly and then cut in half, height-wise, through the middle, as if cutting a "hat" off.
3. Open the lid of the squash and scoop the seeds from the seed cavity.
4. Measure out 2 cups winter squash.
5. Place the winter squash, 1 cup water and coconut milk into a food processor or blender and puree till smooth, about 20 to 30 seconds. Set aside.
6. Into a medium-size saucepan, pour the remaining 1/2 cup water. Sprinkle the surface with the gelatin. Allow the gelatin to dissolve on the surface of the water for 1 minute.
7. Turn the burner heat to medium and stir the water and gelatin. While stirring, add the winter squash puree and continue stirring to mix and fully dissolve the gelatin.
8. After about 3 minutes, the mixture will be steaming but not yet simmering. Turn off the heat.

9. Add the oil, honey, cinnamon, ginger and stevia. Stir the mixture to blend it completely.

10. Pour the filling into the prepared, cooled crust and refrigerate for a minimum of 6 hours, or overnight.

Traditional Baked Pumpkin Pie

(dairy-free)

Sweet Nut Crust

2 cups cashews, macadamia nuts, pine nuts or walnuts, sprouted and dehydrated

2 tablespoons xylitol (Global Sweet brand recommended) or coconut sugar (or 1/16 teaspoon powdered stevia — NuNaturals brand recommended)

4 tablespoons coconut oil, melted

pinch sea salt

Yields 1 pie crust.

Preheat oven to 350 degrees Fahrenheit.

1. Prepare crust first, allowing it time to cool while you prepare the filling.
2. Place the nuts into the work bowl of a food processor.
3. Process until the nuts are as small as you prefer — ideally, some will be powdered and some small pieces will remain — but not long enough to create a nut butter.
4. Add coconut oil, optional sweetener and stevia.
5. Pulse the coconut oil into the nuts until a crumble texture has formed and no large pieces of coconut oil remain.
6. Press nut mixture into a 9-inch pie plate, creating an even, firm crust, up the sides of the pan, too, pushing down on the top side edges so they are smooth and neat. Scallop them slightly, if desired.
7. Bake crust for 8 to 10 minutes, until it is browned slightly and fragrant.

8. Set it aside to cool while you prepare the filling.

Pumpkin Pie Filling

2 cups baked kabocha or butternut squash (see Appendix 2: Methods)

1/4 cup honey, maple syrup, coconut sugar or xylitol (Global Sweet brand recommended) (optional if stevia is used — but if you omit this extra sweetener, increase stevia by 1/16 teaspoon)

2 eggs, preferably grass-fed

1/4 cup coconut cream or homemade nut butter

1 teaspoon cinnamon

1/2 teaspoon ginger

1/4 teaspoon each: allspice, cloves and nutmeg

1 teaspoon vanilla

1/8 teaspoon powdered stevia (or 8 to 10 drops liquid stevia —NuNaturals brand preferred)

Yields filling for 1 pie.

1. Place all ingredients into a blender and puree until smooth, 30 to 40 seconds.
2. Pour pie filling into prepared crust and bake until sides of filling are puffed, golden and starting to crack. The middle of the pie should barely be set, just past its wobbly quality.
3. Remove from the oven. Cool the pie on a metal cooling rack. Chill it for 3 hours or overnight.
4. Serve plain, with whipped cream, lightly sweetened cultured cream or whipped coconut cream.

Chocolate Maple Pecan Pie

(dairy-free)

Boy howdy, this is one mean, good pie! A customer favorite, it can also be made in bar form by baking it in a rectangular or square pan. Sprouted walnuts make a great substitution for the pecans. (Oh, and did I mention it's easy? *Fast* and easy!)

Cashew Pastry Crust

2 cups cashew flour (measured from 4 cups cashews, pureed into a meal in the blender)

1 whole egg, preferably grass-fed

1 egg yolk

2 tablespoons coconut oil

1/4 teaspoon sea salt

Yields 1 pie crust.

Preheat oven to 325 degrees Fahrenheit.

1. Prepare crust first, allowing it time to cool while you prepare the filling.
2. Place the nut flour in an empty blender. Add other ingredients.
3. Process, pulsing as necessary, until the ingredients are evenly mixed, and the texture of the crust is crumbly but sticking together well. A ball will begin to form.
4. Dump out the contents of the blender into your pie plate and press the dough evenly over the surface of the pie plate and up the sides.

5. Bake the crust for 8 to10 minutes, just until it begins to show golden spots and puffed subtle bubbles in places. Cool the crust slightly while you prepare the filling. (If a large bubble forms early on in the baking of the crust, pop the bubble with the point of a sharp knife.)

Chocolate Maple Pecan Filling

2 cups sprouted, dehydrated pecans or walnuts

1 cup pure maple syrup

3 eggs, preferably grass-fed

1/2 cup cocoa

3 tablespoons coconut oil

1 teaspoon vanilla

Yields filling for 1 pie.

1. Place maple syrup, eggs, cocoa, coconut oil and sea salt into a blender and puree until smooth, 20 to 30 seconds.
2. Pour filling into the warm crust. It will be very runny. Move around any nuts to fill the crust evenly.
3. Carefully transfer the pie to the oven and bake until the edges of the filling are puffed and cracked and the middle is just set.
4. Allow pie to cool on a wire rack. Chill 3 hours or overnight, and serve.

Blackberry (or Apple) Pie

(dairy-free, egg-free)

Plan ahead: Making the crust first and placing it in the freezer to chill will prevent it from becoming soggy while the fruit filling sets up inside of it.

Date Nut Crust

3/4 cup cashews

3/4 cup sprouted walnuts

1-1/2 cup dates, cut into 1-inch pieces

1/4 teaspoon sea salt

Yields 1 pie crust.

1. Combine all of the crust ingredients in a food processor or high-powered blender, and pulse to blend.
2. Press evenly into the sides and bottom of a pie plate.
3. Freeze for at least 1 hour while the filling begins to set.

Blackberry (or Apple) Filling

5 cups blackberries, fresh or frozen (and thawed), or

6 cups apples, peeled and thinly sliced

1 teaspoon vanilla for the blackberry pie, or 2 teaspoons for the apple pie

1/2 teaspoon cinnamon (only for apple pie)

1-1/2 cups room-temperature water

1 tablespoon + 2 teaspoons sustainably sourced gelatin

1/8 teaspoon stevia or 1/4 cup honey

Yields filling for 1 pie.

1. Combine the first 3 ingredients in a large bowl: fruit, vanilla and optional cinnamon.
2. Place water and stevia or honey in a medium-large saucepan and sprinkle gelatin over the top.
3. Allow gelatin to dissolve on the water's surface for 1 minute.
4. Cook apple slices in the sweet water for 5 to 10 minutes until they are fork tender.
5. Move cooking pot to the refrigerator until the mixture is cooled slightly, but not yet beginning to set, about 1 hour.
6. If using berries, pour the slightly cooled stevia-gelatin water over the berries and stir thoroughly.
7. Place bowl in the refrigerator for 20 minutes or more so the berry juices can begin to set up. You want the gelatin to thicken; but don't let it set up all the way.

8. Once filling is cooled and is no longer too liquidy, pour the filling into the prepared frozen crust.

9. Using your fingers, reserve or pull out pristine fruit to decorate the top of the pie.

10. Refrigerate pie for 3 to 6 hours, or overnight. Garnish apple pie with a drizzle of pure maple syrup. Garnish berry pie with a drizzle of honey. Serve with Vanilla Bean Crème Fraiche, (Page 179), whipped cream, ice cream or vegan ice cream.

Chocolate Cream Pie

(dairy-free)

If you are a chocolate lover, like I am, this pie will satisfy. It is deep, rich and completely delicious.

2 cups cashews, soaked and wet (see Appendix 2: Methods)

2 cups water

1 tablespoon sustainably sourced gelatin

3/4 cup cocoa, depending on taste preference (use 2/3 cup for a less-dark version)

8 egg yolks, preferably grass-fed (save the whites for another recipe!)

1/4 cup sweetener of choice: honey, maple syrup, coconut sugar or xylitol (Global Sweet brand recommended)

1 tablespoon vanilla

1/8 teaspoon sea salt

1/8 teaspoon stevia, or 2 dropperfuls, to taste (optional; if you are allergic to stevia or would rather not use it, increase the sweetener of choice to 1/3 cup)

Yields 1 pie.

1. Prepare the Cashew Pastry Crust (Page 104), and allow it to cool after baking it blind* while you make the filling.
2. Place the first 3 ingredients in the blender in the order they are listed: cashews, water, then the gelatin sprinkled over the top. Allow the gelatin to dissolve on the surface of the water for 1 minute.
3. Add cocoa.
4. Blend on medium-high speed for about 50 seconds.
5. Pour chocolate milk into a small-medium saucepan and heat over medium heat, stirring consistently so the gelatin doesn't scorch on the bottom of the pan.
6. The gelatin will be dissolved completely when the mixture is steaming but not yet simmering, about 3 to 4 minutes.
7. Remove it from the heat and allow it to cool for 15 minutes.
8. Return the cooled chocolate milk to the blender and add the remaining ingredients: egg yolks, sweetener, vanilla, sea salt and optional stevia.
9. Blend the mixture until well mixed, about 20 seconds.
10. Pour filling into the prepared crust and transfer the pie to the refrigerator.
11. Chill for 6 hours, or overnight.
12. Eat plain or garnish with shaved, unsweetened chocolate, whipped cream or berries.

*Baking a pie crust "blind" simply means baking the pie crust empty, without the filling.

Lemon Meringue Pie

This recipe is dedicated to our 6-year-old son, Julian, because he is our Mozart of recipes, and often his compositions have something to do with Lemon Meringue Pie.

1/2 cup honey

1/2 cup fresh lemon juice

1/4 cup + 2 tablespoons coconut oil, melted and cooled, or room-temperature butter

2 whole eggs, preferably grass-fed

2 egg yolks

2 teaspoon sustainably sourced gelatin

sprinkle of lemon oil, or 1/2 teaspoon fine lemon zest

1 Cashew Pastry Crust (Page 104), baked and cooled slightly

Yields 1 pie.

1. In a high-powered blender, cream the honey and coconut oil or butter, for about 50 seconds on medium speed.
2. In a small bowl, beat together the whole eggs and the egg yolks.
3. Start the motor running again on your blender.
4. Slowly add eggs and egg yolks pouring them into the running blender; blend another 50 seconds.
5. In a medium saucepan, sprinkle gelatin over the lemon juice, and allow the gelatin to dissolve for 1 minute.
6. Add honey-egg puree and lemon oil or zest and stir to mix.

7. Heat the whole mixture gently over low heat, stirring for up to 15 minutes, never letting it simmer.

8. When it's hot and smooth, and when it coats the back of a wooden spoon, it is finished. It will continue to thicken in the fridge. (There should not be any curdling of the eggs with this method. However, if there is, pour custard through a fine mesh sieve before pouring it into prepared crust and refrigerating it.)

9. Pour filling into the prepared crust and refrigerate it while you make the meringue topping.

Honey-Meringue Pie Topping

1 cup local raw honey

4 egg whites, at room temperature

1 tablespoon lemon juice, or 1 teaspoon vanilla

1/4 teaspoon sea salt

1/8 teaspoon powdered stevia (or 10 drops liquid stevia — NuNuturals brand preferred) (optional)

Yields 4 cups.

1. Simmer honey over medium heat until it darkens in color — the "hard ball" stage. (If you drop a bit in some cold water, it will form a firm ball between your finger and thumb, but still be malleable if pressed firmly.) This will take about 10 minutes.

2. Place egg whites in the bowl of a stand mixer (or a metal mixing bowl that you use with your hand-held mixer).

3. Add sea salt and stevia.

4. When honey is ready, bring the saucepan over to the mixer and start the mixer motor on medium speed.

5. As eggs start to froth, turn the mixer up to high speed and add the honey slowly, in a thin stream.

6. Some of the honey will spatter around the edges; (the spatters can be folded in at the end and it's okay if some spatters are too sticky and remain on the sides of the bowl).

7. As meringue volumizes, add your flavoring of choice, (lemon juice or vanilla), and continue mixing it to expedite its cooling, 2 to 3 minutes more.

Final Assembly

1. Remove lemon curd pie from the refrigerator and top it artistically with the meringue. You can pile it all in a big heap and make swirling patterns, or pipe desired patterns from a pastry bag.
2. Chill 3 to 6 hours before serving.

Raw Strawberry-Lemon Cream Pie

(raw, dairy-free, egg-free)

This recipe was shared with me by Andrea Wyckoff of www.LowStarchPaleo.com. Andrea is devoted to providing healing and delicious recipes — and her photographs are inspiring. I am grateful to have a working friendship with such a talented healing-food entrepreneur, and I hope you enjoy checking out her website and Facebook page. You'll love this recipe. Zucchini is used most creatively, and the pie is beautiful.

Raw Crust

3/4 cup sprouted walnuts
3/4 cup dried unsweetened coconut
6 medjool dates, pits removed
2 tablespoons extra-virgin coconut oil
1/4 teaspoon sea salt

Yields 1 pie crust.

1. Use a food processor to process the walnuts, dried coconut and sea salt into a crumbly consistency.
2. Add in the dates (pits removed), coconut oil and sea salt, and process again.
3. Push the sticky crust mixture together in a spring-form pan (lined with waxed or parchment paper). I like to use a 6-inch pie pan, but you can also use an 8-inch pie pan for a flatter, more tart-like pie.

Cream Pie Filling

1 cup zucchini (peeled and chopped)

1/2 cup raw macadamia nuts (or cashews), soaked, rinsed and still wet (see Appendix 2: Methods)

1/2 cup extra-virgin coconut oil, melted

4 tablespoons local raw honey (or coconut nectar)

4 tablespoons lemon juice

1 teaspoon vanilla

pinch sea salt

Yields about 2-1/2 cups.

1. Blend cream pie ingredients together in a high-speed blender (or food processor).
2. Pour cream filling over the pie crust and put the pie into the freezer for 2 hours, or until firm.

Fruit Topping

2 cups fresh strawberries, sliced (or other fresh fruit — pineapple works great, too)

1. Pull pie from the freezer a few minutes before serving and top with fresh fruit.

Note: This cream pie freezes really well, and it will stay delicious for up to a month when stored in the freezer.

cakes & frostings

CHAPTER SIX

Cakes and Frostings

Mercy, let there be cake and frosting! Stand at the counter and eat it; then you won't have to ask for seconds. From a sheet-style treat with thick ganache to a lavishly layered confection for special occasions, cake is the frosting of life.

Chocolate Cake with Chocolate Frosting

1-3/4 cups cashews, soaked and still wet (or substitute walnuts or pine nuts) (see Appendix 2: Methods)

1/2 cup ghee, grass-fed butter or coconut oil, melted and cooled

1/2 cup cocoa

1/2 cup maple syrup (or your preferred sweetener)

2 eggs, preferably grass-fed

1/4 cup flaxseed meal

1 teaspoon cinnamon (optional)

1/8 teaspoon sea salt

1/4 cup coconut flour

1/4 teaspoon baking soda

Serves 8.

Preheat oven to 325 degrees Fahrenheit.

1. Prepare a 9-inch-by-13-inch pan — or two 8- or 9-inch round or square cake pans: Spray them with coconut oil or wipe them with preferred saturated fat, and line them with parchment paper. Spray or coat the paper with fat again. Set aside.

2. Place the first 8 ingredients into a high-powered blender or food processor: cashews, fat, cocoa, sweetener, eggs, flaxseed meal, cinnamon and sea salt.

3. Puree on medium-low speed for 50 seconds, until the puree is smooth and the ingredients are well incorporated.
4. Sift together the coconut flour and baking soda in a small bowl.
5. Add the dry ingredients to the wet ingredients and process until thoroughly distributed; do not over-mix.
6. Pour batter into prepared pan(s) and bake until a toothpick or knife inserted in the center comes out clean or with dry crumbs adhering, about 25 to 45 minutes, depending upon pan size.
7. Cool completely before frosting.

Chocolate Ganache Frosting

Whatever you put under this ganache people will want to eat!

1 cup cocoa

1 cup maple syrup (honey may be substituted, but the ganache will become runny at room temperature; so it's only ideal for preparations that will stay in the fridge until being served)

1/2 cup coconut oil, ghee or grass-fed butter, melted and cooled

pinch of sea salt

Yields about 2 cups.

1. Place all ingredients in a medium-size mixing bowl, and whisk them together thoroughly.
2. In a cool kitchen, the ganache will "set up" and thicken on its own. To expedite the process (or for warmer kitchens), place the bowl in the refrigerator and stir it periodically, every 5 to 10 minutes, until it's reached an ideal spreading consistency. Alternatively, place the set-up ganache in a piping bag. This frosting pipes beautifully — it's great for cupcakes or decorative embellishments.

Chocolate Frosting

(xylitol-sweetened)

This frosting provides the perfect ganache for those who can't have honey or maple syrup.

1/2 cup cocoa

1/3 cup water

1/4 cup xylitol (Global Sweet Brand recommended)

pinch of sea salt

1/2 cup coconut oil, ghee or grass-fed butter (butter will create a less-thick frosting, except when fully refrigerated)

1/2 cup coconut cream, spooned from the top half of the can or skimmed from high-fat, homemade, chilled coconut milk

1/8 cup sprouted nut butter (see Appendix 2: Methods)

1 teaspoon vanilla

1/16 teaspoon powdered stevia (optional)

Yields about 2 cups.

1. Combine water and xylitol in a small saucepan over low heat.
2. Stir or whisk until the xylitol has fully melted.
3. Add cocoa and sea salt, and whisk until the cocoa is completely incorporated.
4. While it's still quite warm, add the remaining ingredients: oil, coconut cream, nut butter, vanilla and stevia.
5. Stir until completely homogenized.
6. Place the bowl in the refrigerator and stir ganache periodically, every 5 to 10 minutes, until it's reached an ideal spreading consistency.

Chocolate Cupcakes

(dairy-free)

Topped with maple syrup-sweetened Chocolate Ganache, these are a top seller at our café — ordered for birthday parties and requested in their absence.

2 cups cashews, soaked and wet (see Appendix 2: Methods)

6 eggs, grass-fed preferred

3/4 cup extra-virgin coconut oil, melted — or olive oil

1/2 cup cocoa

1/4 cup dates

1/4 cup maple syrup

1/4 teaspoon sea salt

1/8 teaspoon powdered stevia (NuNaturals brand preferred) (optional)

1/3 cup flaxseed meal

1/4 cup chia seed meal

1/2 teaspoon baking soda

Yields 8 large or 20 regular-size cupcakes.

Preheat oven to 325 degrees Fahrenheit.

1. Grease muffin tin(s), line them with parchment paper squares, and grease them again. Set aside.

2. Place the first 8 ingredients into a high-powered blender or food processor: cashews, eggs, oil, cocoa, dates, sweetener, sea salt and stevia.

3. Puree on medium speed for about 50 seconds, until the puree is smooth and the ingredients are well incorporated.

4. Sift together the flaxseed meal, chia seed meal and baking soda in a small bowl.

5. Add the dry ingredients to the wet ingredients and process until thoroughly distributed; do not over-mix.

6. Scoop batter into prepared tin(s) and bake until a toothpick or knife inserted in the center comes out clean or with dry crumbs adhering — about 15 to 25 minutes, depending on the tin size(s).

7. Cool completely before frosting.

Chocolate Beet Cake

(dairy-free)

Best served with Chocolate-Avocado-Date Pudding Frosting (see below), this cake is great in a 9-inch-by-13-inch Pyrex pan — not fancy, just comfort food. With the Chocolate-Avocado-Date Pudding Frosting, you will be eating classic chocolate cake but with a whole heap of fun and hidden nutrition.

1 cup cashews, blended into flour

3/4 cup cocoa

3/4 cup maple syrup

1/2 cup coconut oil, melted and cooled

4 eggs, preferably grass-fed

1/4 cup cashews, blended into flour

1/2 teaspoon baking soda, sifted

1/4 teaspoon sea salt

1 cup grated beets

Serves 9.

Preheat oven to 325 Fahrenheit.

1. Grease a 9-inch-square pan or a 9-inch by 13-inch Pyrex pan with coconut oil or ghee. Set aside.
2. Place the first 5 ingredients in a blender, food processor or mixing bowl: cashew flour, cocoa, maple syrup, coconut oil and eggs.

3. Blend until well mixed.

4. In a small separate bowl, whisk together the remaining dry ingredients.

5. Blend the dry ingredients into the wet batter thoroughly without over-mixing.

6. Fold in beets.

7. Pour batter into prepared pan.

8. Bake for 30 minutes, or until a toothpick or sharp knife inserted into the center of the cake comes out clean.

9. Allow cake to cool completely before frosting. This cake is great frosted and refrigerated, eaten the second day after it is made.

Chocolate-Avocado-Date-Pudding Frosting

(dairy-free, egg-free, raw, vegan)

Our family likes to eat this on leftover waffles — like a piece of toast with jam, but a whole lot more decadent and healthy! Wow, dessert and nutrition in the same snack — that's exciting! It's also an excellent frosting on the Chocolate Beet Cake. It can be made with or without the honey.

1 extra-large avocado, or 2 small ones

8 dates, chopped into smaller pieces

1/2 cup cocoa

1/4 cup extra-virgin coconut oil, melted over low heat

1/4 cup honey or maple syrup (optional)

1/16 teaspoon powdered stevia (or 10 to 15 drops liquid stevia — NuNaturals brand preferred)

2 teaspoons vanilla

Yields about 2 cups.

1. Combine all ingredients in a food processor or high-powered blender, scraping down the sides of the bowl as necessary.

2. Use a spatula to scrape the contents into a serving bowl. Serve, or chill until ready to serve.

Carrot Cake

This cake pairs nicely with Classic Cream Cheese Frosting or dairy-free "Cream Cheese" Frosting (recipes follow). It is my kids' favorite dessert recipe.

6 eggs, preferably grass-fed

1 cup hazelnut flour made from 2 cups roasted hazelnuts, (set aside any flour that remains)

3/4 cup coconut oil, ghee, butter or olive oil

1/2 cup flaxseed meal

1/3 cup sweetener of choice: maple syrup, honey or xylitol (Global Sweet Brand recommended)

1/4 cup dates, chopped into small pieces

1-1/2 teaspoons cinnamon

1/4 teaspoon sea salt

1/8 teaspoon stevia (NuNaturals brand preferred)

1/8 cup coconut flour

1/2 teaspoon baking soda

1 cup fresh carrots, grated

1/2 cup fresh pineapple, diced

1/4 cup unsweetened, dried coconut

Yields 1 single-layer, 9-inch cake. The cake can be sliced in half, height-wise, to make a double layer cake with frosting in the middle, as well as on top. Or use multiple small round pans for a multi-tiered cake, as shown in the photograph.

Preheat oven to 350 degrees Fahrenheit.

1. Prepare a 9-inch round or square cake pan: grease it, line the bottom with parchment paper cut to size, and grease the pan again. Set aside.
2. Combine in a food processor the first 9 ingredients: eggs, hazelnuts, oil, dates, flaxseed meal, sweetener, cinnamon, sea salt and stevia.
3. Blend until creamy, about 1 minute.
4. In a small bowl, sift together the coconut flour and baking soda.
5. Add sifted dry ingredients to wet ingredients and blend again for 10 seconds, or until thoroughly incorporated.
6. Immediately add grated carrot, pineapple and coconut; fold it in quickly and briefly.
7. Pour batter into prepared pan, smoothing out the top evenly.
8. Bake until a toothpick inserted in the center comes out clean or with dry crumbs adhering.
9. Cool completely before frosting.

Classic Cream Cheese Frosting with Honey

Double this recipe to make a layer cake.

1 8-ounce package organic cream cheese, at room temperature (Nancy's brand preferred because it's fermented)

1/2 cup extra-virgin coconut oil, melted and cooled

1/4 cup local, raw honey

Yields about 2 cups.

1. Place all 3 ingredients in a mixing bowl and beat with a handheld mixer until they are evenly mixed. Use a spatula to scrape down the sides of the bowl once or twice.

2. Place frosting in the refrigerator briefly, stirring and checking it regularly, until a spreadable consistency is achieved.

3. Frost cake once it has fully cooled.

"Cream Cheese" Frosting

(dairy-free)

Aw, the magic of the cashew — ever creamy in texture and flavor, helping out those of us who can't have dairy. Double the recipe for a layer cake.

1-1/2 cups cashews, soaked 2 hours in warm water, then rinsed

1/2 cup filtered water

3 tablespoons extra-virgin coconut oil

2 tablespoons local raw honey, (or substitute stevia to taste, or 6 to 8 soaked dates*)

1 tablespoon vanilla

1/4 teaspoon sea salt

Yields about 2 cups.

1. Puree all of the ingredients until completely smooth.
2. Transfer to a small bowl and refrigerate until a firmer, spreadable consistency is achieved.

*Cover dates with hot water for 2 hours. Strain off water and proceed with recipe.

Zucchini Spice Chocolate Cake

(dairy-free, stevia-sweetened option)

This versatile recipe can be sweetened with only stevia, or with the added sweetener, or with no stevia and only the added sweetener, depending on dietary needs or allergies. It can be made as big muffins, in any shaped cake pan, or in a loaf pan. The cinnamon and cloves both help with insulin production and make this an extra-healthy way to have dessert or a sweet snack.

2 cups cashews or sprouted walnuts

1 cup grated zucchini

4 eggs, preferably grass-fed

1/2 cup extra-virgin coconut oil or extra-virgin olive oil

1/3 cup honey, maple syrup, coconut sugar or xylitol (Global Sweet Brand recommended) (optional)

1/4 cup cocoa

2 teaspoons vanilla

1 teaspoon cinnamon

1/4 teaspoon cloves

1/4 teaspoon sea salt

1/8 teaspoon powdered stevia (or 15 drops liquid stevia — NuNaturals brand preferred) (optional if other sweetener is used)

1/3 cup flaxseed meal

1/2 teaspoon baking soda

Serves 6 to 10, depending upon pan size.

Preheat the oven to 325 degrees Fahrenheit.

1. Prepare a muffin tin, a 9-inch round or square cake pan, or a loaf pan by lining it with parchment paper and greasing the paper with preferred fat.
2. Place the first 11 ingredients in the blender: nuts, zucchini, eggs, oil, optional sweetener, cocoa, vanilla, cinnamon, cloves, sea salt and stevia.
3. Blend on medium speed until batter is smooth, about 50 seconds.
4. In a small bowl, sift together the flaxseed meal and baking soda.
5. Start the motor of the blender and add the dry ingredients through the door in the lid. Process only long enough to evenly incorporate the baking soda, without over-mixing — about 10 to 15 seconds.
6. Pour batter into prepared pan and bake for 25 minutes for large cupcakes, 35 minutes for a 9-inch cake, or 50 to 60 minutes for a loaf, until batter is well-puffed, golden, crispy at the edges, and a knife inserted in the center comes out clean or with a few dry crumbs adhering. Check the cake before the designated time to be sure it doesn't over-bake.
7. Remove cake(s) from the oven and allow to cool completely.
8. Serve this moist cake alone, unadorned, or with the one of the following fabulous toppings: Chocolate Ganache Frosting (Page 119), Chocolate-Avocado Pudding Frosting (Page 124) or Chocolate Crème Fraiche (Page 176)

Apple Cake

(xylitol-sweetened)

Guests will never know they are eating a grain-free, sugar-free cake.

1-1/2 cups almonds, soaked and wet, or 2 cups walnuts, soaked and wet (see Appendix 2: Methods)

6 eggs, preferably grass-fed

1/2 cup melted coconut oil or fat of choice

1/2 cup hardwood-derived xylitol (Global Sweet Brand recommended)

1/3 cup flaxseed meal

1 teaspoon vanilla

1 teaspoon cinnamon

1/4 teaspoon sea salt

1/4 cup coconut flour

1/2 teaspoon baking soda

1 cup diced Granny Smith apple

Serves 6 to 10, depending upon pan size.

Preheat the oven to 325 degrees Fahrenheit.

1. Prepare a muffin tin, a 9-inch round or square cake pan, or a loaf pan by lining it with parchment paper and greasing the paper with preferred fat.

2. Place the first 8 ingredients in the blender: nuts, eggs, oil, sweetener, flax, vanilla, cinnamon, and sea salt.

3. Blend on medium speed until batter is smooth, about 50 seconds.

4. In a small bowl, sift together the coconut flour and baking soda.

5. Start the motor of the blender and add the dry ingredients through the door in the lid. Process only long enough to evenly incorporate the baking soda, without over-mixing — about 10 to 15 seconds.

6. Fold in the apples by hand, using a spatula.

7. Pour batter into prepared pan and bake for approximately 35 minutes for a 9-inch cake, until batter is well-puffed, golden, and a knife inserted in the center comes out clean or with a few dry crumbs adhering. Check the cake before the designated time to be sure it doesn't over-bake.

Hazelnut "Buttercream" Frosting

(dairy-free)

1 cup sprouted, dehydrated hazelnuts

1/2 cup extra-virgin coconut oil

2 tablespoons honey, maple syrup, or hardwood-derived xylitol (Global Sweet brand recommended), stirred into 2 tablespoons boiling water to dissolve

Yields about 2 cups.

1. Blend nuts in a blender or food processor until they become a fine meal, just beginning to turn into nut butter around the edges.
2. Add coconut oil.
3. Blend again, using a spatula as necessary to scrape down the sides and corners.
4. Finally, add the sweetener or the xylitol-sweetened water and blend until the ingredients are evenly incorporated.
5. Pour frosting into a medium-size bowl and refrigerate it, stirring every 5 minutes — for about 20 minutes total — until a spreadable consistency is achieved.
6. Frost the cooled cake. Garnish cake with whole hazelnuts.

Cashew "Buttercream"

(xylitol-sweetened)

2 cups cashews, soaked and wet (see Appendix 2: Methods)

1 cup coconut oil, melted and cooled, or ghee

1/2 cup room-temperature water

1/4 cup xylitol (Global Sweet brand preferred)

2 egg yolks, preferably grass-fed

1 teaspoon sustainably sourced gelatin

1 teaspoon vanilla

1/8 teaspoon freshly ground nutmeg

1/8 teaspoon cinnamon

1/8 teaspoon stevia

teeny pinch sea salt

Yields about 3 cups.

1. Place water in a small saucepan and sprinkle the gelatin over its surface.
2. Allow gelatin to dissolve for 1 minute.
3. Add xylitol.
4. Heat water over medium heat, stirring the entire time, as the gelatin dissolves completely.
5. When water-xylitol mixture is steaming but not yet simmering, turn off the heat and allow it to cool slightly.
6. Place *all* ingredients in a high-powered blender and process on medium speed for about 50 seconds, until frosting is completely smooth.
7. If texture and thickness is right, frost your cooled cake at this point; or transfer the frosting to a bowl and refrigerate it briefly, stirring the edges into the center from time to time, until the desired stiffness is achieved. Watch the frosting closely to prevent it from setting up too much. If this happens, simply melt it down slightly again, stir and refrigerate, until you have reached the right temperature and texture.

Cashew "Buttercream"

(dairy-free, stevia-sweetened)

This frosting is not overly sweet. But the texture offers the sublimity one would expect from any buttercream. It's exciting to have a stevia-sweetened frosting that is so versatile and so delicious! I love the almost savory flavor, like sweet butter on cake.

2 cups cashews, soaked and wet (see Appendix 2: Methods)

1 cup coconut oil, ghee or butter, melted and cooled

1/8 + 1/16 teaspoon powdered stevia (NuNaturals brand recommended)

1/2 cup room-temperature water

1 teaspoon sustainably sourced gelatin

2 egg yolks, preferably grass-fed

1 teaspoon vanilla

1/8 teaspoon freshly ground nutmeg

1/8 teaspoon cinnamon

teeny pinch sea salt

Yields about 2-1/2 cups.

1. Place water in a small saucepan and sprinkle gelatin over its surface.
2. Allow gelatin to dissolve for 1 minute.
3. Heat water over medium heat, stirring the entire time, as the gelatin dissolves completely.
4. When water is steaming but not yet simmering, turn off heat and allow it to cool slightly.
5. Place all the ingredients in a high-powered blender and process on medium speed for about 50 seconds, until the frosting is completely smooth.
6. Frost your cooled cake at this point. Or transfer the frosting to a bowl and refrigerate it briefly, stirring the edges into the center from time to time, until the desired stiffness is achieved. Watch the frosting closely to prevent it from setting up too much. If this happens, simply melt it down slightly again, stir and refrigerate until you have reached the right temperature and texture.

Variation:

- Add 2 tablespoons honey or maple syrup, if tolerated, for a sweeter buttercream.

easy eggs, clafouti and porridges

CHAPTER SEVEN

Easy Eggs, Clafouti and Porridges

For simple breakfast meals, satisfying and easy to prepare, turn to this chapter. The inventiveness of these recipes will surely keep you on your toes, even while they unite us with our ancestors in their humble nature.

Berry Clafouti

(stevia-sweetened)

Here's another use for egg whites after you've used the yolks in custard, ice cream, eggnog, etc. Traditional for dessert, often served with cheese, clafoutis also make kids smile when you serve them for breakfast. The surprise here is that this clafouti contains no sugar, is full of protein and good fat, yet still tastes like a treat!

1-1/2 cups soaked wet nuts or seeds, (or 3/4 cup dehydrated — both methods work) (see Appendix 2: Methods)

7 to 8 egg whites, preferably grass-fed (the recipe is versatile and works with either amount of whites; so use more for more protein or less if you have fewer on hand or are in a hurry)

3/4 cup extra-virgin coconut oil, ghee or grass-fed butter, melted

2 tablespoons coconut flour, (or use 1/4 cup coconut flour, if using dehydrated nuts)

1/8 teaspoon powdered stevia (or 15 drops liquid stevia — NuNaturals brand preferred)

1/8 teaspoon sea salt

1/2 teaspoon baking soda, mixed with 2 tablespoons water

2 cups berries, fresh or frozen

Serves 9.

Preheat oven to 325 degrees Fahrenheit.

1. Grease a 9-inch square pan with coconut oil or ghee.
2. Place first 6 ingredients together in the blender: egg whites, oil, nuts, flour, stevia and sea salt.
3. Blend on medium-high speed for about 30 seconds, until the puree is smooth.
4. Keeping the blender motor running, dump in the baking soda-water mixture all at once.
5. Puree an additional 5 to 8 seconds, until thoroughly incorporated.
6. Fold in berries now, or sprinkle them over the batter once in the pan.
7. Pour the batter into the prepared pan, and sprinkle the berries evenly over its surface if choosing this option.
8. Bake for 30 to 35 minutes, until a toothpick or knife inserted into the cake comes out clean, or with dry crumbs adhering.
9. Serve alone, with dry, aged cheese — or with a custard, whipped cream or ice cream on top. For breakfast, top with fully cultured yogurt or cream.

Variations:

- Substitute any fruit in season for the berries — chopped, diced or sliced and arranged decoratively. Consider using the lowest sugar option: Granny Smith apple (peeled for this recipe, unless it's diced).

- Add 1 teaspoon cinnamon to the batter before pureeing.

- For a no-fruit option, fold 2 cups chopped rhubarb into the batter. Add 2 tablespoons honey or other sweetener, if tolerated.

- Omit baking soda if you need to protect the pH of your stomach for optimum digestion.

Steamed Eggs

I love a simple breakfast that is nourishing and easy. We make this dish on our warm woodstove, which allows us an extra-low-fuss preparation; we just ignore the eggs while they cook! The lowest heat on your stovetop also will produce a great finished product. This recipe has no nuts, flour, seeds, etc. It is ultra-simple and appropriate, — even for the GAPS Introduction Diet, with a mug of bone broth on the side — and it's super easy to digest.

Serves 1. Multiply ingredients for number of servings desired.

2 eggs per person

1 whole raw zucchini per person, roughly chopped

1/8 teaspoon sea salt per person

rendered animal fat or ghee

1. Place the first three ingredients into a blender.
2. Blend on medium speed for 30 seconds, or until zucchini is completely pureed.
3. Place a frying pan on your woodstove or over low heat on your stovetop. Choose the frying pan size based on how many servings you are preparing. Use a teeny pan for just 1 serving or a large frying pan if you are serving 4 or more people.
4. Melt a generous amount of fat in the pan, 2 to 3 teaspoons per person — no more than 2 tablespoons total. Rotate pan to distribute fat evenly, coating the bottom, and up the sides to some extent.
5. Pour puree into greased pan and cover with a lightly greased lid. The eggs and zucchini will actually steam over this low heat.

6. Peek at eggs after 5 minutes, making sure that the heat is low enough that they don't brown too much on the bottom.* After 15 to 20 minutes, it will be puffed, with small air pockets throughout. If you are busy, the "soufflé" can stay on a warm woodstove for 10 additional minutes, just to keep it easy and warm.

7. Serve.

*If your stovetop does not provide a low enough heat and the eggs are browning on the bottom too much, transfer them to a 300-degree-Fahrenheit oven after the initial 5 to 10 minutes.

Marshmallow Root and Slippery Elm Porridge for One

(egg-free, stevia-sweetened)

This is an egg-free breakfast that is versatile according to your diet. The herbs have healing, soothing properties, as well as being anti-inflammatory. Their flavor? Healthy, grassy but also comforting and creamy, like baby food, rice cereal or a good-for-you Cream of Wheat. Many of the recipes in this book are indulgent tasting. This one is not. It is cozy health food.

3/4 cup milk of choice (raw dairy milk, coconut milk, or homemade nut or seed milk), warmed but not hot

1 tablespoon slippery elm

1 tablespoon marshmallow root, blended to a powder and sifted so there are no stringy, grassy pieces

1 tablespoon chia seeds

1/4 teaspoon cinnamon

pinch of powdered stevia (or 5 drops liquid stevia — NuNaturals brand preferred)

Serves 1.

Toppings:

- Local raw honey, to taste, if tolerated
- Crispy nuts, to taste, if tolerated (see Appendix 2: Methods)
- Fresh berries or dried goji berries, if fruit is tolerated; blueberries recommended

1. Stir all the ingredients together in your serving bowl and cover.
2. Allow chia seeds to expand and soften for 10 minutes.
3. Top with optional toppings.
4. Enjoy!

AIP Variation:

- Omit chia seeds and increase slippery elm and marshmallow root to 1-½ tablespoons each.

Sweet Collard Greens Porridge with Blueberries

(dairy-free option, egg-free, nut-free, stevia-sweetened)

This porridge is green. Topped with fresh or frozen blueberries, the color contrast screams healthfulness and fun, and invites you to taste the undiscovered flavor. Surprisingly, just as kale goes great in green smoothies that contain fruit, collards have a clean, subtle, minty flavor that complements blueberries. The flavor of the hot cereal itself is nutty and similar to unsweetened oatmeal — a wee bit bitter, as some grains are, but a comforting palette for cream, fruit and sweetener. This porridge can be sweetened only with stevia for those who are fructose sensitive. Enjoy this breakfast adventure!

4 cups filtered water

1 cup raw hemp seeds

1/8 teaspoon powdered stevia (or 15 drops liquid stevia, NuNaturals brand preferred)

5 large leaves from collard greens, lower stems cut away where the leaf begins, and discarded

2/3 cup chia seeds

Serves 4.

1. In a high-powered blender, combine water and hemp seeds.
2. Add stevia and process on medium-high speed for 50 seconds. Do not strain. The milk is now ready to use.
3. Set aside some of the milk for topping the porridge so that the amount that remains in the blender is 3 cups.
4. Add broad collard leaves to the blender, pushing them down a bit toward the blade.
5. Puree for 50 seconds on medium speed until the greens are fully pureed and the milk is bright green. (The brightness of the hue varies depending on the time of year and the batch of collards.)
6. Pour milk into a medium-size saucepan and heat gently, stirring, over medium heat till the mixture is steaming hot but not yet simmering.
7. Turn heat off and add chia seeds, stirring well immediately to avoid clumping. Allow the seeds to thicken the porridge for 10 full minutes.
8. Stir in half of the blueberries.
9. Serve porridge, topping each bowl with additional berries and making honey, maple syrup or additional milk available as optional toppings.

Toppings:

- 2 cups fresh or frozen blueberries
- Local raw honey or organic maple syrup, to taste (optional)
- Hemp milk or grass-fed cream, to taste

Winter Squash Porridge

(dairy-free, egg-free, stevia-sweetened)

Fit to serve guests, this is a welcome change for breakfast. It's a bit like warm pumpkin pie filling — a wholesome, nourishing version. You can bake the winter squash the night before, or use leftover squash to expedite breakfast.

3 cups cooked winter squash

1 cup room-temperature water (amount will vary depending on density and variety of winter squash; use as little as possible to obtain the porridge consistency desired)

1/4 cup extra-virgin coconut oil

1 tablespoon sustainably sourced gelatin

1/2 teaspoon cinnamon

1/8 teaspoon sea salt

1/8 teaspoon powdered stevia (or 15 drops liquid stevia — NuNaturals brand preferred)

Serves 4.

1. Add water to blender and sprinkle gelatin over the surface.
2. Add remaining ingredients: winter squash, coconut oil, cinnamon, sea salt and stevia.
3. Puree on medium speed for 20 seconds, or until the mixture is smooth. Pop any air bubbles near the blade with your spatula, stopping and starting the blender once or twice. If necessary, add more water — 1/2 cup at a time — to make the blender run smoothly.
4. Transfer puree to a large saucepan.
5. Heat puree over medium heat, stirring for 5 to 10 minutes.
6. Allow mixture to simmer briefly, and then remove it from the heat.
7. Serve porridge topped with shredded unsweetened coconut, sprouted "crispy" nuts, optional cream, honey or maple syrup.

Variations:

- Add a fried egg on top for a savory variation, and for added protein and good cholesterol. Use bone broth in place of water for an even more savory version.
- Add a pat of butter on top.
- Chill porridge, or any leftovers, for a gelatin snack. My kids love this! Topped with coconut in individual glasses, it's pretty.

savory breads, pizza, rolls and casseroles

CHAPTER EIGHT

Savory Breads, Pizza, Rolls and Casseroles

Now, let's realize that there is a time for sweets, and there is a time to abstain and tip our hat to savory foods. They are SO good! I am a happy camper with these rich foods on my table. But please forgive the irony that the first recipe of this chapter contains chocolate. What can I say?

Sweet Sandwich Rolls, or Bittersweet Chocolate Sandwich Rolls

(stevia-sweetened)

Wonderful fillings for these kid-friendly rolls include Sprouted Nut Butter (see Appendix 2: Methods) and fruit, Raw Jam (Page 201), and aged cheese for those who can have dairy. My 13-year-old daughter also recommends peanut butter and bacon. And my newly-able-to-eat-cheese 11-year-old son recommends peanut butter and gouda cheese. To each his own. I vote "yes" for all these options!

2 cups raw cashews, soaked and wet (or use pine nuts if cashews are a problem) (see Appendix 2: Methods)

1/2 cup extra-virgin coconut oil, ghee or rendered animal fat

2 eggs, preferably grass-fed

1/4 cup chia seeds

1/4 cup flaxseed meal

2 teaspoons vanilla

1/8 teaspoons powdered stevia (or 10 to 15 drops liquid stevia — NuNaturals brand preferred)

1/8 teaspoon sea salt

1 ounce unsweetened chocolate, minced or shaved finely (optional)

1 tablespoon coconut flour

1/2 teaspoon baking soda

Yields 25 teeny rolls for an afternoon tea party or finger food — or 10 larger rolls for more traditional sandwiches.

Preheat oven to 350 degrees Fahrenheit.

1. Lightly grease 2 baking sheets — or line them first with parchment paper, then grease and set aside. (Coconut oil spray can be a good tool for this step.)
2. In a high-powered blender, blend chia seeds, eggs and fat on medium speed for 30 seconds, until chia seeds split and the mixture is creamy, yellow and thickened.
3. In a small bowl, sift together the coconut flour and baking soda.
4. Scrape contents of blender into a food processor and add the cashews, flaxseed meal, vanilla, stevia and sea salt. Process until mostly smooth — about 1 minute.
5. Add optional chocolate and dry ingredients.
6. Process, pulsing briefly but thoroughly, until dry ingredients are evenly incorporated, without over-mixing.
7. Use an auto-scoop or two spoons to create your desired-size, roll-shaped mounds and place them onto the prepared baking sheet.
8. Bake until puffed and a toothpick comes out of the center clean (or with a few dry crumbs adhering) — about 15 minutes for the mini rolls, or 30 minutes for the larger.

Variation:
- Use walnuts or macadamia nuts in place of the cashews.

Loaf Bread, for Sandwiches or Not

6 eggs, preferably grass-fed

2 cups cashews, walnuts or other favorite nuts, soaked and wet (see Appendix 2: Methods)

1/2 cup coconut oil, ghee or butter, melted

1/2 cup chia seeds

heaping 1/4 teaspoon sea salt

1/4 cup flaxseed meal

1/2 teaspoon baking soda

Serves 8 to 10, depending on the thickness of the slices.

Preheat oven to 325 degrees Fahrenheit.

1. Prepare a loaf pan by lining it with parchment paper and greasing the paper with preferred fat.
2. Place first 5 ingredients into a blender: eggs, nuts, oil, seeds and sea salt.
3. Blend on medium speed until the batter is smooth — about 50 seconds.
4. In a small bowl, sift together the flaxseed meal and baking soda.
5. Start motor of the blender and add dry ingredients through the door in the lid. Process only long enough to evenly incorporate the baking soda, without over-mixing — about 10 seconds.
6. Pour batter into prepared loaf pan and bake for 45 to 60 minutes — until well-puffed, golden brown, crispy on its surface and a knife inserted in the center comes out clean or with a few dry crumbs adhering.
7. Remove loaf from oven and allow it to cool.
8. To slice cooled bread, pull up on both sides of the parchment paper, removing it from the loaf pan.

Panini

6 eggs, preferably grass-fed

2 cups nuts or seeds of choice, soaked and wet (see Appendix 2: Methods)

3/4 cup extra-virgin olive oil or preferred fat, melted and cooled

heaping 1/4 teaspoon sea salt

1/8 teaspoon powdered stevia (or 10 to 15 drops liquid stevia — NuNaturals brand preferred)

2 tablespoons water

1/2 teaspoon baking soda

1/3 cup flaxseed meal

1/4 cup chia seeds

Serves 8 to 9.

Preheat oven to 325 degrees Fahrenheit.

1. Lightly grease 2 baking sheets — or line them first with parchment paper, then grease and set aside. (Coconut oil spray can be a good tool for this step.)
2. Place first 5 ingredients into a high-powered blender: nuts, eggs, olive oil, sea salt and stevia. Blend on medium-high speed until batter is smooth — about 50 seconds. (A traditional blender will work too; even if the nuts or seeds don't get as smooth, the recipe will turn out well.)
3. In a separate bowl, stir together water and baking soda.
4. Pour wet ingredients into a medium-size mixing bowl.
5. Add baking soda water, flaxseed meal and chia seeds. Use a mixer to blend the final ingredients into the thickening batter briefly but thoroughly.
6. Allow batter to set up for 10 minutes.
7. Scoop panini batter onto prepared cookie sheets, preferably using a 3- or 4-ounce ice cream scoop with an automatic-release mechanism.
8. Bake 25 to 30 minutes, until panini are puffed in the center, golden brown on top, and light brown around the edges. A toothpick or sharp knife inserted into the center should come out clean, with no wet batter adhering.
9. Cool 10 minutes on baking sheets before removing panini to baking racks. Once cool, slice panini horizontally and use for sandwich bread.

Kale Panini Variation:

1. Follow the above recipe, but add 1 cup loosely packed kale to the initial wet ingredients.
2. To the final ingredient step with baking soda, add an additional 1/4 cup chia seeds, for a total of 1/2 cup chia seeds; increase the flaxseed meal to a total of 1/2 cup.

Yorkshire Pudding "Polenta" Cake

Brazil nuts really have their place. They offer not only a unique nutritional profile, being higher than most foods in selenium, but also a unique texture that, when pureed, lends itself particularly well to certain recipes. This high-fat, savory cake is excellent for those craving British comfort food. Served with a roast or a burger, you can make a theme of it: roasted veggies, a lovely salad, maybe a bit of cheese and some beer if you can have it. Me, I like the cake the next day too; any excuse to eat fatty bread. Mmm … . Use a great big cast-iron skillet if you have one, preferably after making burgers or a roast in it; the meat drippings will further flavor and enhance the savory cake.

1-1/2 cups soaked Brazil nuts, wet (see Appendix 2: Methods)

6 eggs, preferably grass-fed

2/3 cup coconut oil or rendered animal fat, not melted, solid and chilled, and chipped off or cut into pea- or marble-size pieces

1/3 cup flaxseed meal

1/2 teaspoon sea salt

heaping 1/8 teaspoon powdered stevia (NuNaturals brand preferred)

1/6 cup coconut flour

1/2 teaspoon baking soda

1/4 cup rendered animal fat, ghee or grass-fed butter

Serves 8.

Preheat oven to 325 degrees Fahrenheit.

1. Over medium heat, melt animal fat in a large cast-iron skillet or oven-ready, broad-bottomed pan or Dutch oven. Roll fat around in the pan so it partially coats the sides. Turn the heat off under the pan.

2. Place first 5 ingredients together in a food processor: nuts, eggs, fat, flaxseed meal and stevia. (Alternatively, if you don't have a food processor, first process the nuts, flaxseed meal and stevia in a blender to create a flour. Then, in a large metal bowl, use two knives to "cut" the fat into the flour mixture. Lastly, stir in the eggs.)

3. Use the pulse button many times to create a lumpy batter.

4. In a small bowl, sift together coconut flour and baking soda.

5. Sprinkle dry ingredients evenly over the batter, and pulse again several times until thoroughly incorporated, without over-mixing.

6. Pour batter into prepared pan.

7. Bake for 30 to 35 minutes, until a toothpick or knife inserted in the cake comes out clean, or with dry crumbs adhering.

Pizza Dough

While most pizza is baked at high temperatures, the precious olive oil in this recipe demands we bake it at a lower temperature, preserving the healthfulness of the ingredients. You may also use avocado oil, if you prefer. Regarding toppings, to each his own favorites. May I recommend, though, Italian prosciutto? When purchasing, look for a product that has only two ingredients: pork and salt. This rich meat is best cut into squares and sprinkled over the finished pizza, so it retains its buttery texture and flavor. Of course, in the summer, fresh tomatoes and basil can't be beat. And wild mushrooms, sautéed with garlic (for those not on an anti-candida diet), are one of life's pleasures worth closing your eyes to enjoy fully.

Preheat oven to 325 degrees Fahrenheit.

1 cup wet almonds (or 1-1/2 cups walnuts or other nuts that have been soaked) (See Appendix 2: Methods)

1 cup extra-virgin olive oil

4 whole eggs, preferably grass-fed

2 egg whites

1 teaspoon basil, oregano or rosemary

1/2 teaspoon sea salt

1/16 teaspoon stevia

3/4 cup chia-seed meal

1/8 cup coconut flour

1/8 cup flaxseed meal

1/2 teaspoon baking soda

Yields 2 thin-crusted 12-inch round pizzas, or 1 larger rectangular pizza.

1. Prepare a round pizza pan by rubbing it with olive oil, coconut oil or animal fat — or spray with coconut oil spray. For a rectangular pizza, prepare a cookie sheet in the same manner, greasing the bottom and sides.
2. Place these ingredients into a high-powered blender in the following order: eggs, olive oil, almonds or other nut, herbs, sea salt and stevia.
3. Blend on medium-high speed until the mixture is batter-like and mostly smooth.
4. Sift together the remaining dry ingredients in a small bowl: chia-seed meal, coconut flour, flaxseed meal and baking soda.
5. Add these to the blender and quickly puree them on medium speed to completely and evenly incorporate them into the batter, without over-mixing.
6. Do not let the batter set up and thicken. Immediately pour the batter into an even round circle on the prepared pan, smoothing out the surface and shape with an offset spatula. Alternately, pour the batter into your prepared cookie sheet, spreading out the batter evenly into the rectangular shape.
7. Bake dough for 15 to 20 minutes, until the edges are drying out and the center is puffed in places.
8. Remove dough and immediately top it with your favorite toppings: homemade tomato sauce, sautéed sausage or lightly cooked bacon, grated aged cheese, feta, goat cheese or homemade, Herbed Dairy-free Ricotta (recipe follows), sautéed onions, bell peppers, olives, fresh garlic, cubes of cooked winter squash, sprouted walnuts, chanterelle mushrooms, etc.
9. Bake pizza for 20 additional minutes, until the edges are brown but not too dark, and the ingredients in the center are sizzling and hot, tinged with brown.
10. Top with optional prosciutto, homegrown tomatoes (in season) and fresh basil; slice and serve.

Herbed Dairy-free Ricotta

2 cups cashews, soaked and wet (see Appendix 2: Methods)

3/4 cup extra-virgin olive oil

1/2 cup mild, all-natural green olives (canned with only olives, water and salt)

1 teaspoon nutritional yeast (optional)

1 teaspoon fresh lemon juice (optional)

1 clove garlic, minced

1/2 teaspoon sea salt

1/2 teaspoon rosemary or oregano

1/4 teaspoon dried basil

1. Place all the ingredients in a high-powered blender and puree on low speed until mixture is smooth — about 1 minute. If necessary, scrape any larger pieces up from the bottom and blend again.

2. Spoon teaspoonfuls all over the pizza when it is ready for toppings — before its second baking.

Beef Stew En Croute

This satisfying casserole doesn't contain baking soda in the crust, making it a great choice for GAPS adherents. Who doesn't love Beef Stew with a crusty bread topping to sop up the juices?

Preheat oven to 325 degrees Fahrenheit.

Filling

1-1/2 pounds beef chuck roast, cut into 1-1/2-inch cubes

1 teaspoon paprika

1 teaspoon white pepper

1 teaspoon oregano

1 teaspoon sea salt

1/2 teaspoon thyme

1/4 cup rendered rendered animal fat, ghee or other animal fat

2 cups onions, roughly chopped

2 cups carrots, sliced diagonally

2 turnips, peeled and cut into 1-inch cubes

3 tablespoons tomato paste (optional)

1 teaspoon sea salt

1 teaspoon thyme

1/2 teaspoon allspice

1. Mix all spices together with a fork on a large plate or in a shallow, broad platter.
2. Toss meat in spices until all sides are coated.
3. Using a Dutch oven or large, heavy cast-iron skillet, melt 1 tablespoon rendered animal fat in the pot over medium-high heat.
4. Add 1/3 to 1/2 of the overall meat to the pan, depending on its size, so it isn't overcrowded (you want the meat to sear, not to steam). Brown meat on all sides, using tongs to turn it — about 5 minutes total for each batch.
5. Add 1 tablespoon of the remaining animal fat and continue to cook the remaining meat in one to two batches. Set aside.
6. Melt remaining 2 tablespoons rendered animal fat in the hot pan and add onions (or greens of green onions if Low-FODMAP) and sea salt. Saute until the onions are translucent and beginning to brown, about 5 minutes.
7. Add thyme and allspice, and sauté for an additional 2 minutes — until spices begin to be fragrant.
8. Add bone broth, optional tomato paste, carrots and turnips.
9. Bring liquid to a simmer, stirring to incorporate tomato paste.
10. Turn heat to low and put the lid on.
11. Simmer on low heat for 20 minutes, until carrots and turnips are fork tender but not mushy. Set aside.

Topping

1 cup Brazil nuts, soaked and dehydrated

6 eggs, preferably grass-fed

1/3 cup coconut oil or rendered animal fat, solid

1/4 cup chia seeds

1/2 teaspoon coriander

1/8 teaspoon sea salt

1/16 teaspoon powdered stevia (NuNaturals brand preferred)

1. Place ingredients together in a food processor: nuts, eggs, fat, chia seeds, coriander, sea salt and stevia. (Alternatively, if you don't have a food processor, process the nuts, flaxseed meal and stevia in a blender to create a flour. Then, in a large metal bowl, use two knives to "cut" the fat into the flour mixture. Lastly, stir in the eggs.)
2. Use the pulse button many times to create a lumpy batter that is well combined without being over-mixed.
3. Set aside.

Casserole Assembly

Serves 6 to 8, depending on portion sizes.

1. Prepare a large casserole dish by rubbing its interior with your fat of choice.
2. Ladle the entire "beef stew" into the casserole dish, using a spatula to scrape the cooking pot clean.
3. Pour batter over stew, using a spatula to spread it evenly over the entire surface. It does not need to touch the sides of the dish.
4. Bake casserole in preheated oven for approximately 35 minutes, until the topping is browned and puffed in the center and the broth-y sides are bubbling wildly.
5. Remove from oven and let cool slightly before serving.

Slow-cooked Pork Cobbler

You will need a large, lidded Dutch oven or cast-iron skillet for this dish — something big enough to hold all the meat, vegetables and the cobbler.

2-1/2 to 3 pounds country-style pork ribs, pork butt or shoulder roast, lightly salted, (bone-in OK)

2 pounds carrots, unpeeled and sliced into bite-size chunks

2 pounds rutabaga, peeled and cut into bite-size pieces

Savory Breads, Pizza, Rolls and Casseroles

1 bunch collard greens, chopped small and steamed until the center ribs are tender

3/4 cup bone broth or homemade broth

2 star anise

2 cardamom pods

2 bay leaves

1/4 cup rendered animal fat, melted

sea salt and pepper, to taste

2 cups cashews, soaked, sprouted and still wet (or other preferred soaked nut or seed) (see Appendix 2: Methods)

6 eggs, preferably grass-fed

3/4 cup rendered animal fat or ghee, melted and cooled

grated zest of 1/2 an orange

1 teaspoon dried parsley (or 1 tablespoon fresh)

1/4 teaspoon sea salt

1/16 teaspoon powdered stevia (or 10 drops liquid stevia — NuNaturals brand preferred)

1/2 cup flaxseed meal

1/2 cup chia seeds, ground to a meal in your blender or coffee grinder

1/2 teaspoon baking soda

Serves 8.

Preheat oven to 300 degrees Fahrenheit.

1. In a large Dutch oven, cast-iron skillet or casserole dish with lid, toss carrots, rutabaga, spices, animal fat, salt and pepper together with two spoons, until the vegetables are well-coated with the fat and salt.
2. Add salted pork and distribute vegetables evenly under and around meat.
3. Place lid on dish and bake for 2-1/2 to 3 hours.
4. Meanwhile, place cashews, eggs, animal fat, stevia and sea salt into a high-powered blender and blend on medium-high speed until the cashews are smooth — about 50 seconds.
5. Add orange zest and parsley, and blend briefly.

6. In a separate bowl, sift together the two kinds of seeds and baking soda.

7. Start motor running on blender again, and quickly add in all dry ingredients. Blend for about 10 seconds, being careful not to over-mix — just until the dry ingredients are evenly incorporated.

8. Allow batter to set up in the refrigerator while the meat and vegetables finish cooking.

9. Remove Dutch oven, check meat for tenderness, and, using two forks or a fork and a knife, break or cut all of the meat into bite-size pieces. Remove any bones. (The meat, when ready, should be very tender, cutting apart easily or falling from the bone.)

10. Add steamed collards and 3/4 cup bone broth, and briefly mix the ingredients together so that they are evenly distributed in the pan.

11. Raise oven temperature to 325 degrees Fahrenheit.

12. Scoop mounded cobbler batter onto the casserole, preferably using a 3- to 4-ounce ice cream scoop with an automatic-release mechanism. Make the scoops decoratively arranged, as desired, overlapping slightly around the perimeter only or spaced apart in a grid-like pattern over the entire surface of the casserole. (Optionally, brush egg yolk on the surface of each biscuit to create a shiny glaze.)

13. Bake 25 to 30 minutes, until cobbler batter is puffed and golden brown. A toothpick or sharp knife inserted into the center of one should come out clean, with no wet batter adhering.

14. Serve immediately, or allow to cool for up to 15 minutes before serving.

Shepherd's Pie

This recipe always brings me back to an Irish pub in San Diego that I enjoyed as a girl with my Daddy, listening to his Irish buddy sing and play the piano as I ate my first ever Shepherd's Pie, which was speckled within with fresh parsley.

2 pounds ground lamb

1-1/2 teaspoons sea salt

2 cloves garlic, smashed and diced

2 teaspoons rosemary

1 teaspoon thyme

1/2 teaspoon nutmeg

1/2 teaspoon white pepper

2 cups onions, roughly chopped

2 tablespoons rendered animal fat, ghee or coconut oil

1/2 teaspoon sea salt

2 cups carrots, sliced diagonally and steamed for 20 minutes

2 cups frozen peas, or fresh and blanched in boiling salted water for 1 minute

1 large bunch fresh spinach, steamed till wilted and chopped roughly

1-3/4 pounds kabocha or butternut squash, baked at 375 degrees Fahrenheit until tender (about 1-1/2 hours) and flesh separated from seeds and skin — or 1-3/4 pounds rutabaga, peeled, cubed and steamed until fork tender

2 turnips, peeled, cubed and steamed until fork tender

3/4 cup coconut oil, ghee or rendered animal fat, melted

1/4 cup fresh parsley

2 egg yolks

1 clove garlic, smashed and chopped

1/2 teaspoon sea salt, to taste

1/4 teaspoon white pepper

Serves 8 to 10.

Preheat oven to 375 degrees Fahrenheit.

1. In a large sauté pan over medium heat, cook the lamb and salt, breaking it into desired bite-size pieces. Cook for 3 to 5 minutes, until most of the pink outside of the meat has darkened, stirring it and breaking it up at regular intervals.
2. Add spices and continue to cook, exposing all the spices to the pan's heat for an additional 2 to 3 minutes, until the spices are fragrant.
3. Empty hot meat to a large plate and set aside. If there is extra fat in the pan, reserve it for use with the onions.
4. Add rendered animal fat, onions and sea salt to the pan and sauté over medium heat for 3 minutes. As onions begin to brown, turn the heat to low and continue to cook for 20 minutes, stirring occasionally.
5. Add carrots, peas and spinach, and stir to coat. Turn heat off and set aside.
6. Place winter squash, turnips, oil, parsley, egg yolks, garlic, sea salt and white pepper into a food processor (or a blender may be used if the mixture is separated into multiple batches so as not to overwork the blender's motor).
7. Puree squash mixture until thoroughly smooth. Taste for salt. Add another 1/4 teaspoon as necessary.

Casserole Assembly

1. Prepare a large casserole dish by rubbing its interior with rendered animal fat, coconut oil or ghee.
2. Ladle onion mixture into casserole dish, using a spatula to scrape the cooking pot clean.
3. Sprinkle lamb and spices over the onions.

4. Pour winter squash batter over the stew, using a spatula to spread it evenly over the entire surface. If it is stiff enough, use the tines of a fork to create a pattern all over the surface of it, as with traditional Shepherd's Pie, like a rake in a sand trap.

5. Bake the casserole in preheated oven for approximately 35 to 40 minutes, until the topping is browned and puffed in the center and the broth-y sides are bubbling wildly.

6. Remove from oven and let cool slightly before serving.

toppings, sauces, custards, puddings and compotes

CHAPTER NINE

Toppings, Sauces, Custards, Puddings and Compotes

My super-duper favorite chapter! These recipes encapsulate all that is rich and flavorful, smooth in texture and unabashedly not subtle. Toppings, sauces, custards, puddings and compotes are always royalty on a spoon. And, because I use them as toppings, I'm including glorious yogurt and ice cream recipes as well.

Chocolate Crème Fraiche

(stevia-sweetened)

When our family first went on the GAPS Diet — and after we had passed through the Valley of the Shadow of the Introductory Diet (just kidding) — this was a favorite comfort food. Nothing is yummier than the simple, pure decadence of dark chocolate and fully cultured cream. The texture of the cream and the intensity of the dark chocolate were pure pleasure dolloped generously on grain-free waffles and garnished with fresh berries. I'm not sure if Dr. Natasha Campbell-McBride would approve, but if you have a streak of Bacchus in you, live it up with this! Stevia makes this a truly sugar-free treat.

2 cups natural, organic sour cream (grass-fed, only a couple of ingredients and fully cultured — such as Nancy's brand)

1/2 cup cocoa

1/2 cup boiling water

1/16 teaspoon powdered stevia (or 10 to 15 drops liquid stevia — NuNaturals brand preferred)

Yields about 2-1/2 cups. This recipe easily doubles or triples.

1. Place cocoa in a small mixing bowl.
2. Add boiling water, and whisk until thoroughly incorporated.
3. Add stevia, and whisk briefly again.
4. Let "ganache" cool to room temperature.
5. Place sour cream in a separate small bowl (or a 4-cup Pyrex measuring cup to make it easier to measure the cream).

6. Add about half the cooled chocolate; whisk until smooth and evenly incorporated.

7. Taste for how chocolate-y you want the finished product. Add more of the dark chocolate accordingly. (I use at least 3/4 of it, depending on the day and my mood.)

8. Finally, adjust the recipe for sweetness, adding more stevia if desired — a little at a time, being careful not to add too much.

9. Serve in large cascading dollops on top of waffles. Any remaining chocolate (that wasn't stirred into the sour cream) can be stirred into coffee — or it will last indefinitely, covered in the fridge, for various cravings and uses.

Variations:

- You may substitute your favorite sweetener for the stevia: Raw honey, pure maple syrup or xylitol can be stirred into the boiling water-cocoa mixture until dissolved. Add more boiling water if necessary, up to an additional 1/4 cup. Start with 1/4 cup sweetener and adjust to taste.

- This recipe can be halved, yielding a generous portion for one person or a modest portion for two to share as a topping.

Chocolate Sauce

This pourable sauce is great on ice cream and can be used as a chocolate sauce anywhere — in coffee, on cake, as a garnish, etc.

1-1/4 cups water, at room temperature

1 cup cocoa

1 cup raw honey, maple syrup or xylitol (Global Sweet brand recommended)

1 teaspoon vanilla

1/8 teaspoon powdered stevia (or 10 to 15 drops liquid stevia (NuNaturals brand preferred) (optional)

pinch of sea salt

Serves 8 to 12.

1. Before heating, whisk together all ingredients in a small to medium-size saucepan until thoroughly mixed.
2. Place over medium heat and stir constantly to dissolve the sweetener and to make the cocoa flavor bloom. Do not simmer.
3. When the mixture is steaming but not yet simmering, remove it from the heat and allow it to cool.
4. It is now ready to serve — or it may be stored, sealed, in the refrigerator for up to one month. Stir it again before serving, as some settling will occur.

Vanilla Bean Crème Fraîche

(stevia-sweetened)

A dollop of this dense perfection will set most things right. Atop pie, layered in a parfait (see Pages 245, 247, 248) or eaten straight, it is a guilt-free indulgence for those who can enjoy grass-fed dairy. Life does that sometimes — gives us pure pleasure that's good for us.

2 cups sour cream (homemade or store-bought organic and grass-fed, fully cultured with only cream, probiotics, prebiotics and sea salt as ingredients — such as Nancy's brand)

1/8 teaspoon powdered stevia (or 15 to 20 drops liquid stevia — NuNaturals brand preferred)

1/8 teaspoon vanilla specks scraped from a cut-open vanilla bean pod, or 1 teaspoon vanilla

Yields 2 cups.

1. Place all 3 ingredients in a small to medium-size- mixing bowl.

2. Whisk together ingredients until they are thoroughly and evenly homogenized.

3. Enjoy!

Russian Crème Fraiche

(stevia-sweetened)

There are times when you want a sweet crème fraiche that will pipe or hold a specific shape, a cultured cream that will stay put, not sink or deflate. If you want a soft, spoonable, gelled cream, use the smaller amount of gelatin (1 teaspoon). For a crème that will hold up to a fork or be cut by a knife atop a pie, use the larger amount.

1/2 cup water, room temperature or cold

1 to 2 teaspoons gelatin, depending on thickness desired

2 cups sour cream (homemade or store-bought organic and grass-fed, fully cultured with only cream, probiotics, prebiotics and sea salt as ingredients — such as Nancy's brand)

1/8 teaspoon powdered stevia (or 15 to 20 drops liquid stevia — NuNaturals brand preferred)

1/8 teaspoon vanilla specks scraped from a cut-open vanilla bean pod, or 1 teaspoon vanilla

Yields 3 cups.

1. Place water in a small saucepan and sprinkle the gelatin over it; allow gelatin to dissolve on the surface of the water, about 1 minute.
2. Over medium heat, stir gelatin water for 2 to 3 minutes, until steam appears above the water, a subtle foam appears on the water's surface and the gelatin becomes clear. The mixture will be hot but not yet simmering.
3. Remove mixture from heat and allow to cool to a warm temperature while you proceed with the next step.

4. Place next 3 ingredients into a medium-size mixing bowl: sour cream, stevia and vanilla specks.

5. Whisk together ingredients until they are thoroughly and evenly homogenized.

6. Pour cooled gelatin water into crème fraiche, whisking constantly.

7. The crème fraiche is now ready to top a pie. To pipe with it, fill a pastry bag and place the bag in the refrigerator for up to 30 minutes. Periodically, try piping a small amount to see if it's chilled to the right consistency. Parfaits and other uses can be applied immediately. The crème fraiche will continue to gel up and become more solid as it refrigerates. A full 3 hours will allow it to gel completely.

Fully Cultured Raw Yogurt

(lactose-free)

It's far easier to make raw yogurt than to make yogurt with pasteurized dairy. You don't have to heat the milk because there are no pathogens to kill, as there would be with pasteurized milk that doesn't have beneficial bacteria to keep bad bacteria at bay! (The pasteurization process kills beneficial bacteria, and also lactase, the naturally occurring digestive enzyme that helps break down or digest lactose, the milk sugar so many of us are "allergic" to. Thus, the importance of eating raw milk products whenever possible.) This tangy yogurt will be runny and full of probiotics. If you want it to set up and be more like store-bought yogurt, never fear: I've got you covered. See the variation below.

1 quart raw milk
2 tablespoons pure starter yogurt (any high-quality plain yogurt, such as Nancy's brand)

Yields 1 quart.

1. Place raw milk in a large ceramic bowl.
2. Stir in a pure starter yogurt until well mixed.
3. Cover and place in a consistently warm area for exactly 24 hours, no less, so that ALL of the lactose is consumed.
4. Add any desired sweetener — such as pure maple syrup or local, raw honey — drizzled over the top. Or stir in stevia, to taste.

Variation:

- Dissolve 1 tablespoon sustainably sourced gelatin over 1/2 cup filtered room-temperature water in a small saucepan. Heat it until the gelatin has fully dissolved, stirring as it heats; do not let the mixture boil. Cool the water. Stir it into the milk and starter before allowing the milk to ferment. Chill the finished yogurt before consuming, allowing the gelatin to set up the yogurt.

Coconut Whipped Cream

(dairy-free, egg-free)

Although I usually like to promote and use completely whole foods, this topping is distinctly made from canned coconut milk. It provides a non-dairy whipped topping that is otherwise not possible. Native Forest brand seems to deliver consistent results. You want full-fat coconut milk, not "lite" versions.

2 cans coconut milk (Native Forest brand recommended)

2 tablespoons raw honey or pure maple syrup — or a few drops liquid stevia, to taste

2 teaspoons vanilla

Yields about 2 cups.

1. Chill cans of coconut milk in the refrigerator overnight.
2. Five minutes before whipping, place your whipping bowl, beaters and the cans of coconut milk in the freezer, being careful not to tip them, which can stir their contents.
3. Remove items from freezer. Open cans and scoop out the solid coconut cream from the top half into your chilled bowl. Reserve the bottom liquid for smoothies or another recipe.
4. Beat the cream until it whips up, volumizing and gaining body, about 3 to 5 minutes.
5. Add sweetener and vanilla during the final 30 seconds of beating.
6. Use immediately, or chill until ready to serve.

Variation:

- For a thicker coconut cream that will have a more solid body, dissolve 2 teaspoons sustainably sourced gelatin over 1/4 cup room-temperature water in a small saucepan. Heat it until the gelatin has fully dissolved, stirring as it heats; do not let the mixture boil. Cool the water slightly. Pour it into the whipping cream in the last 30 seconds of beating. Chill the finished coconut cream before consuming, allowing the gelatin to firm it up.

Vanilla Custard

(dairy-free)

This decadent classic is texture sublimity. You can use the custard while still warm if you want it to be pourable, like Crème Anglaise. Or you can chill it if you want it to set up and be scoopable, for filling crepes or serving in individual glasses.

2 cups water

1 cup pine nuts or cashews, soaked, sprouted and still wet (see Appendix 2: Methods)

1/8 teaspoon powdered stevia (or 15 to 20 drops liquid stevia — NuNaturals brand preferred)

scant pinch of sea salt

8 eggs yolks, preferably grass-fed

1 tablespoon sustainable gelatin

1 tablespoon sweetener of choice: honey, maple syrup, coconut sugar or xylitol (Global Sweet brand recommended)

1/2 teaspoon vanilla

Yields about 3-1/2 cups.

1. Combine first 4 ingredients in a high-powered blender: water, pine nuts, stevia and sea salt. Puree on medium-high speed for 1 minute. (This blend creates the best milk ever!)
2. Pour 1 cup of the milk into a small saucepan, reserving the rest in the blender.
3. Sprinkle gelatin over the surface of the liquid.

4. Heat over medium heat, stirring, for 2 minutes, until steam forms and the gelatin dissolves, but the water has not yet simmered.
5. Remove saucepan from the heat and allow it to cool slightly — about 10 minutes.
6. Add gelatin water back into the blender with the remaining ingredients: egg yolks, sweetener and vanilla.
7. Blend on medium speed for 30 seconds.
8. Serve warm or chilled, either in individual serving dishes or in one larger serving dish. To chill, allow the custard 3 hours to set up.

Hemp Scoopable Custard with Whole Raspberries

(dairy-free, stevia-sweetened)

This is a very special recipe. Rolled up inside grain-free Crepes, (Page 27) and topped with a drizzle of the warm custard, this dish can be served for breakfast, brunch or as a substantial dessert after a light meal. It's amazing that it's only sweetened with stevia because it really is beautiful and soul-satisfying. That's the magic of no-sugar treats: they leave you feeling happy, not longing for more. Have fun with the process of making this one, too! In what seems like a sleight-of-hand trick, the frozen raspberries make the custard gel almost instantly — liquid to solid in a matter of minutes. Delicious and rewarding.

2-1/2 cups hemp milk (next recipe)

1/4 cup coconut oil

4 egg yolks, preferably grass-fed

1 tablespoon + 2 teaspoons sustainably sourced gelatin

1/8 teaspoon powdered stevia (or 15 to 20 drops liquid stevia — NuNaturals brand preferred)

10 to 12 ounces frozen organic raspberries

Serves 4.

1. Measure 2-1/2 cups from the homemade hemp milk.
2. Place 1 cup of it into a small saucepan.

3. Sprinkle gelatin evenly over the surface of the milk. Wait 1 minute for it to dissolve. (Use a spoon to stir it in if the milk's foam is creating a barrier.)

4. Heat milk gently over medium-low heat, stirring constantly, until the mixture is steaming but not yet simmering, and the gelatin has dissolved into the milk.

5. Set aside the hot milk to cool slightly.

6. Pull the frozen raspberries out of the freezer and pour them into a medium-size serving bowl.

7. Pour the slightly cooled milk into the blender with the room-temperature milk. Add coconut oil and egg yolks.

8. Blend contents briefly, until the oil is melted and the ingredients are well blended — about 15 seconds.

9. Pour 3/4 of the total custard over the frozen raspberries and stir patiently. The frozen raspberries will react with the gelatin, and the mixture will gradually solidify. Once it is very thick and custard-like, after 1 to 2 minutes of stirring, place it in the refrigerator until you are ready to serve.

10. Reserve the remaining custard in the blender as a garnish, for drizzling over the finished dish.

Variation:

- For a sweeter custard, add 2 tablespoons raw honey or other sweetener of choice.

Hemp Milk Recipe

(dairy-free, stevia-sweetened, vegan)

3 cups filtered water

2/3 cup raw hemp seeds (sometimes called hemp hearts)

1/8 teaspoon powdered stevia (or 15 to 20 drops liquid stevia — NuNaturals brand preferred)

Yields 4 cups.

1. Place all ingredients in a high-powered blender. Blend on medium-high speed for 50 seconds. Do not strain the milk.
2. Use the milk "as is" for this custard recipe. For other purposes, see the variations below.

Variations:

- Add up to 2 tablespoons cocoa.
- Use 3/4 cup hemp seeds for a thicker milk.
- Add 1/2 teaspoon cinnamon for a Horchata-style milk that is tasty and great for blood sugar.

Traditional Blintz Filling

1-1/2 cups cottage cheese (raw and homemade or store-bought — such as Nancy's brand, which is cultured), or ricotta cheese

4 ounces cream cheese (such as Nancy's brand, which is cultured), at room temperature

3 tablespoons local raw honey, maple syrup or hardwood-derived xylitol (Global Sweet brand recommended)

1 egg, preferably grass-fed

Yields 8.

1. Combine all ingredients in a high-powered blender or food processor on the lowest speed.
2. Blend until smooth, or until the ingredients are evenly incorporated.
3. Use to fill Crepes (Page 27): Place about 1/3 cup filling into each crepe and roll up burrito-style.
4. Line up the crepes on a greased baking pan or in a large, shallow casserole dish, seam-side down.
5. Bake at 325 degrees Fahrenheit for 25 minutes, until toasty, golden brown on the outside and filling is hot on the inside.
6. Serve with Mixed Berry Compote (Page 199), Raw Jam (Page 201), fresh berries, fully-cultured sour cream, or Granny Smith Applesauce (Page 16), with homemade sausage patties on the side.

Dairy-Free Blintz Filling

(dairy-free, stevia-sweetened)

2 cups cashews, soaked and still wet (or substitute pine nuts or macadamia nuts)

1-1/4 cups homemade nut, seed or coconut milk (see Appendix 2: Methods)

3 tablespoons local, raw honey, or 1/8 teaspoon powdered stevia (or 15 to 20 drops liquid stevia — NuNaturals brand preferred)

2 tablespoons coconut oil, melted and cooled, or sustainably sourced lard

1 egg, preferably grass-fed

2 teaspoons vanilla, 2 teaspoons lemon zest, or 1 teaspoon cinnamon

1/4 teaspoon sea salt

Yields 3-½ cups.

1. Combine all ingredients in a high-powered blender or food processor.
2. Blend until smooth, or until ingredients are evenly incorporated.
3. Use to fill crepes: Place about 1/3 cup filling into each crepe and roll up burrito-style.
4. Line up crepes on a greased baking pan or in a large, shallow casserole dish, seam-side down.
5. Bake at 325 degrees Fahrenheit for 25 minutes, until toasty, golden brown on the outside and filling is hot on the inside.
6. Serve with Mixed Berry Compote (Page 199), Raw Jam (Page 201), fresh berries, fully-cultured sour cream, or applesauce (Page 16), with homemade sausage patties on the side.

Vanilla Date Shake "Ice Cream"

(dairy-free, vegan)

This recipe hearkens back to my childhood in Carlsbad, California, which was full of sunshine and a well-known fruit and nut stand that made memorable date shakes. This updated version is dedicated to my Daddy, who worked in Carlsbad for more than 50 years and who loves ice cream, and to my Mum, who raised me on coconut frozen yogurt and who loves this flavor particularly. We offer this flavor in our Whiteaker District scoop shop in Eugene. It's a Paleo flavor — no sugar, no grains, just whole foods coming together to make a sweet treat.

2 14-ounce cans full-fat coconut milk, or 3-1/2 cups homemade high-fat coconut milk (see Beverages, Page 213)

3/4 cup dates

1/2 cup boiling water

1/2 cup maple syrup or preferred sweetener of choice: honey, coconut sugar or xylitol (Global Sweet brand recommended)

2 teaspoons vanilla

Serves 4.

1. Place dates in a small, heat-proof bowl.
2. Add boiling water and allow to sit for 20 minutes, until the dates are softened and the water has cooled slightly.
3. Place mixture in a high-powered blender with the remainder of the ingredients: coconut milk, maple syrup and vanilla. Blend until the ingredients are as smooth as your blender will allow — about 50 seconds.
4. Pour mixture into an ice cream maker and freeze according to the manufacturer's instructions.

Dark Chocolate "Ice Cream"

(dairy-free, vegan)

To convey how sublime this ice cream really is, I will share that on my last night before starting the no-sugar GAPS Diet, I sat in my office doing paperwork, eating mini after mini of the organic sugar version of this ice cream. (Minis are the name we give to the smallest size at our ice cream shops.) At that time, we had this flavor in our soft-serve machine, and it was chocolate perfection, even for a dairy lover. Serve this decadent, satisfying, dairy-free ice cream on a waffle, on its own, wrapped inside a crepe, or with sprouted walnuts sprinkled on top. Also great with berries or Mixed Berry Compote (Page 199). I guess I thought I would just have one mini, but then I couldn't stop.

- 2 14-ounce cans full-fat coconut milk, or 3-1/2 cups homemade high-fat coconut milk (see Beverages, Page 213)
- 1 cup sweetener of choice: honey, maple syrup, coconut sugar or 3/4 cup xylitol (Global Sweet brand recommended)
- 1/2 cup cocoa (not Dutch process)
- 1/2 cup boiling water
- 2 teaspoons vanilla

Serves 4.

1. Place cocoa in a small heatproof bowl.
2. Add boiling water and whisk until well mixed. Allow to cool for 15 minutes.
3. Place coconut milk, cooled cocoa "ganache," sweetener and vanilla in a blender. Puree until smooth, scraping down the sides if necessary.
4. Freeze in an ice cream maker, according to the manufacturer's instructions.

The Best Frozen Yogurt

(lactose-free)

2 cups kefir or plain yogurt, (preferably homemade and fully cultured for 24 hours, or a high-quality store-bought variety, such as Nancy's brand)

1 cup natural* grass-fed sour cream (such as Nancy's brand), or unfermented grass-fed heavy cream, if tolerated

3/4 cup sweetener** of choice: raw honey, pure maple syrup, coconut sugar or 2/3 cup xylitol (Global Sweet brand recommended)

1 teaspoon vanilla

Serves 4.

1. Puree kefir and sweetener in a blender until the sweetener has dissolved — 30 to 50 seconds.

2. Add cream and vanilla, and blend very briefly — just until ingredients are blended.

3. Pour mixture into an ice cream maker and freeze according to manufacturer's instructions.

Variations:

- Many other flavors can be made with just a little creativity, keeping the basics the same: 3/4 teaspoon mint extract and shaved dark or unsweetened chocolate, stirred in after the final blending, makes Mint Chocolate Chip.

- Omit vanilla for a true Crème Fraiche flavor.

- For lemon flavor, add 1/2 cup fresh lemon juice and 1 tablespoon lemon zest, or a few drops of lemon oil.

- Eggnog is a favorite flavor in our family: Add 8 grass-fed raw egg yolks to the kefir, as well as 1/2 teaspoon cinnamon, 1/4 teaspoon nutmeg and an optional 1/8 cup rum.

*When buying organic sour cream, always read the list of ingredients. It should only have a few: cream, salt, probiotic. If it has a big long list of ingredients, you can be sure that it isn't fully cultured either, nor is it health food.

**Stevia will not work in this recipe.

Carrot Cinnamon Frozen Yogurt

(lactose-free)

This is a favorite spring flavor in our shops.

2 cups cultured cream (such as Nancy's brand sour cream)

1 cup fresh carrot juice

3/4 cup honey or maple syrup, or 2/3 cup xylitol (Global Sweet brand recommended)

1 teaspoon vanilla

1/2 teaspoon cinnamon

Serves 4.

1. Place all ingredients into a blender and puree until the ingredients are homogenized, or until the sweetener is fully dissolved — 50 seconds or less.
2. Pour mixture into an ice cream maker and freeze according to manufacturer's instructions.

Variation:

- For an AIP non-dairy variation, use 2 cups coconut milk in place of the cultured cream.

Straight-up Ice Cream

I learned to make ice cream from Ben and Jerry. I received their cookbook from two separate people on separate occasions. It was meant to be. Really, their principles for basic ice cream making exceed all other ice cream recipes. I have taken their principles to a new level, making them without sugar. But I owe so much to these two food lovers. Ironically, it is also the fact that I was eating too many pints of Ben & Jerry's that led us to open our own healthy kefir-based frozen yogurt shop. I was afraid I'd die early from heart disease if I kept eating that much sugar, and cream that wasn't grass-fed. Still, they were great revolutionaries for their time, rejecting corn syrup in their ice cream bases and making such unusual and fun, gourmet flavors.

Almost four years into my healing process, I was able to reintroduce cream and maple syrup. This is the recipe that welcomed me back. It is knock-your-socks-off good.

2 cups grass-fed heavy cream

1 cup filtered water (yep!)

2/3 cup pure maple syrup, or local raw honey

2 raw, grass-fed egg yolks (optional, but highly recommended)

1 tablespoon real vanilla extract

Serves 4.

1. Place water, maple syrup, egg yolks and vanilla into a blender. Puree briefly until the ingredients are well mixed — about 15 seconds.
2. Add the cream, and process again very briefly — about 5 seconds.
3. Pour the mixture into an ice cream maker, as directed by the manufacturer.

Cranberry-Mixed Berry Compote

(honey or stevia sweetened)

A favorite topping in our ice cream shop, this is also great on waffles or layered in parfaits.

2 cups frozen or fresh local cranberries

2 cups fresh or frozen local blueberries

1-1/2 cups sliced strawberries

1-1/2 cups marionberries or blackberries

1-1/2 cups raspberries

1/2 cup fresh* blueberries (optional)

1/2 cup honey (or for a stevia-sweetened version, substitute the same amount of freshly pressed apple juice)

1/4 cup freshly pressed apple juice or water

1/4 cup lemon juice

1/8 teaspoon powdered stevia (or 15 drops liquid stevia, NuNaturals brand preferred)

Serves 20.

1. Stir cranberries, juice or water, and honey (if using) over medium heat to dissolve the honey.
2. Simmer until cranberry skins just begin to pop/burst/split.
3. Allow cranberry mixture to cool slightly.
4. Place blueberries, lemon juice and 2/3 of the cooled cranberry mixture into a blender, and blend until smooth.

5. In a large bowl, combine remaining ingredients with the blender puree: strawberries, marionberries, raspberries, remaining whole-cranberry sauce and fresh blueberries.

6. It is now ready to serve. Or cover and refrigerate the compote. It keeps well for five to seven days.

*Most berries may be fresh or frozen with good results. And not all the different kinds of berries must be included; use what is available. Three kinds total is fine. Both the variety and overall quantity of berries stirred in at the end are flexible. However, if you stir in blueberries at the end, they are much better if fresh, texture-wise. The quantity of fresh or frozen berries you stir in will affect the outcome and nature of the sauce, but it will taste great either way.

Three toppings from left to right: Mixed Berry Compote, Peanut Butter Sauce and Xylitol Chocolate Ganache

Raw Jam

(stevia-sweetened option)

2 cups summer berries (fresh, or frozen and defrosted)

6 dates (optional if fructose-sensitive)

2 tablespoons chia seeds

1/16 teaspoon powdered stevia (or 5 to 10 drops liquid stevia, NuNaturals brand preferred)

Yields 2-½ cups.

1. Combine all of the ingredients in a food processor or high-powered blender until the dates are very small.
2. Transfer to a small bowl or jar with lid and refrigerate until ready to serve.

Chocolate-Avocado Pudding

(dairy-free, egg-free, raw, vegan)

2 ripe avocados (preferably the buttery Bacon or Fuerte avocados, which have a less-strong avocado flavor but an amazing fat profile and texture)

1/2 cup cocoa powder

1/2 cup honey or pure maple syrup

1/4 cup extra-virgin coconut oil, melted

1 teaspoon vanilla

Yields 3 cups.

1. Combine all ingredients in a food processor or high-powered blender, scraping down the sides as necessary.
2. Pour pudding into individual pudding dishes, and top with optional toppings (see "Variations" below). Chill for at least 1 hour, or until ready to serve. This is best served the day it is made.

Variations:

- Top the pudding with Lily's stevia-sweetened chocolate chips, shaved unsweetened chocolate, unsweetened shredded coconut, hemp seeds, goji berries or fresh strawberries.

- Line a small loaf pan with parchment or wax paper and spread the pudding inside. Top with chocolate chips and freeze for 1 hour. Cut into cubes and serve immediately as fudge.

- Top the pudding or the fudge with gray or pink sea salt, to taste.

Blender Chocolate Mousse

(dairy-free)

Simply put, this is one of my favorite things to eat in the whole world. If you add extra gelatin, you can fill a homemade piecrust with it and be very happy indeed with the results. Chill and top with dairy or coconut whipped cream for Chocolate Cream Pie (Page 109). Served alone in ramekins or pretty glasses, or topped with fresh strawberries or raspberries, you have a perfect, simple, classic, killer-good dessert.

2 cups soaked wet cashews (see Appendix 2: Methods)

2 cups water

2 teaspoons sustainably sourced gelatin

2/3 to 3/4 cups cocoa, depending on taste and color preferences—whether you like dark or milk chocolate

8 egg yolks, preferably grass-fed (save whites for another recipe!)

1/4 cup sweetener of choice: honey, maple syrup or xylitol (Global Sweet brand recommended)

1 tablespoon vanilla

1/8 teaspoon sea salt

1/8 teaspoon powdered stevia (or 15 drops liquid stevia — NuNaturals brand preferred) (optional; if you are allergic to stevia or would rather not use it, increase sweetener of choice to 1/3 cup)

Serves 6.

There are two ways to make this recipe. If you have a Blendtec blender you can simply put all the ingredients in the blender and run it on the soup setting two times in a row, and the mousse will be done. It is a noisy business, but shockingly fast to deliver such elegant perfection. If you don't have a Blendtec, follow these instructions:

1. Place the first 3 ingredients in the blender in the order they are listed: cashews, water, then the gelatin sprinkled over the top. Allow the gelatin to dissolve on the surface of the water for 1 minute.
2. Add cocoa.
3. Blend on medium-high speed for about 50 seconds.
4. Pour chocolate milk into a small to medium-size saucepan and heat over medium heat, stirring consistently so the gelatin doesn't scorch on the bottom of the pan.

    The gelatin will be dissolved completely when the mixture is steaming but not yet simmering.
5. Remove from the heat and allow it to cool for 15 minutes.
6. Return cooled chocolate milk to the blender, and add the remaining ingredients: egg yolks, sweetener, vanilla, sea salt and optional stevia.
7. Blend mixture until well mixed, about 20 seconds.
8. Serve warm as a sauce, or chill to serve as a mousse. Poured into individual pretty glasses, the mousse can be topped with fresh berries, whipped cream and/or shaved chocolate.
9. Definitely lick the spatula.

Marionberry "Yogurt"

(dairy-free, stevia-sweetened, vegan)

2 cups soaked, wet cashews (see Appendix 2: Methods)

1 cup water, or Beet Kvass to add probiotics, (recipe on Page 218)

1/2 teaspoon vanilla

1/8 teaspoon or less powdered stevia (or 10 to 15 drops liquid stevia — NuNaturals brand preferred)

1 cup frozen marionberries

Serves 4.

1. Place all ingredients except frozen berries in a high-powered blender.
2. Puree until smooth on a low speed, increasing the speed as the motor will allow.
3. Add berries and process until desired texture is obtained.
4. Serve alone or with baked goods.

Note: If you add probiotics in the form of Beet Kvass, be sure to refrigerate the yogurt. Otherwise, the sugar in the berries will ferment and create alcohol. This recipe is best eaten the day it is made.

Strawberry-Walnut Pate

(dairy-free, stevia-sweetened, vegan)

1 cup walnuts, soaked and still wet (see Appendix 2: Methods)

1 cup strawberries (not frozen)

1/4 cup extra-virgin coconut oil, melted and cooled

1/8 teaspoon powdered stevia (or 15 drops liquid stevia — NuNaturals brand preferred)

1/8 cup chia seeds

Serves 4.

1. Place first 4 ingredients into a high-powered blender or small food processor: walnuts, strawberries, coconut oil and stevia.
2. Blend until mixture is smooth, stopping the motor and scraping down the sides as necessary.
3. Fold in the chia seeds with a spatula and set aside, allowing the pate to set up and thicken.
4. Serve inside sliced-open Sweet Sandwich Rolls (Page 152) to make protein-rich "Whoopie Pies."
5. Eat pate the first day. It doesn't keep well.

Pumpkin Butter with Strawberries

(dairy-free, egg-free, stevia-sweetened)

2 cups baked kabocha squash (instructions follow), or one 14-ounce can BPA-free, organic pumpkin

1 cup water

1/4 cup extra-virgin coconut oil (or ghee or grass-fed butter)

1/2 cup water, at room temperature

2 teaspoons sustainably sourced gelatin

1-1/2 cups strawberries, sliced

1 teaspoon cinnamon

1/8 teaspoon powdered stevia + optional additional 1/16 teaspoon (or 15 to 20 drops liquid stevia — NuNaturals brand preferred)

Serves 4 to 6.

Preheat oven to 375 degrees Fahrenheit.

1. Bake kabocha squash for 1-1/2 hours, or until very tender when poked deeply with a knife.
2. Allow it to cool slightly and then cut in half, height-wise, through the middle, as if cutting off a "hat."
3. Open the lid of the squash, and scoop the seeds from the seed cavity.
4. Measure out 2 cups winter squash.

5. Place winter squash and 1 cup water into a food processor or blender and puree until smooth, about 20 to 30 seconds. Set aside.

6. Into a medium-size saucepan, pour 1/2 cup water. Sprinkle surface with the gelatin. Allow gelatin to dissolve on the surface of the water for 1 minute.

7. Turn burner heat to medium, and stir the water and gelatin. While stirring, add the winter squash puree and continue stirring to mix and fully dissolve the gelatin.

8. After about 3 minutes, the mixture will be steaming, but not yet simmering. Turn off heat.

9. Add strawberries, cinnamon and stevia. Stir to blend completely.

10. Add coconut oil and stir to blend again.

11. Serve warm over waffles, pancakes or another favorite baked good. Or use chilled inside a piecrust or individual small dishes.

Peanut Butter Sauce

(vegan)

I am not quiet about recipes that I really like. It is not for a lack of humility, but simply an incredible enthusiasm for good food. When I make something I like, I talk about how good it is because I am so excited that it is hard for me to be quiet. My family is very accepting of this idiosyncrasy, and I hope that you will be, too. This is the best peanut butter sauce in the whole world! It is great on ice cream, great on anything, great by itself. Just try to think of more ways to use it because if you love peanut butter, it will make you happy.

1-1/2 cups coconut milk

3/4 cup maple syrup, raw local honey, coconut sugar or xylitol (Global Sweet brand recommended)

1/2 cup peanut butter

1/2 cup water

1/4 cup coconut oil

1 teaspoon vanilla

1/4 teaspoon sea salt

1/4 teaspoon cinnamon

Yields 3-½ cups.

1. Steadily stir all of the ingredients in a medium-size saucepan over medium heat until they are homogenized and the "sugar" is melted. Cool.

2. Layer with soft homemade ice cream (to create a swirl effect when it is scooped) before freezing the ice cream hard in the freezer; or make it part of a sundae bar. This recipe is SOOO good layered with vegan Dark Chocolate Ice Cream (Page 194).

Note: This sauce keeps refrigerated for 1 month, but it will solidify. If you wish to use the sauce as a sauce after it's been chilled, simply heat it gently to melt, stirring occasionally, and then allow it to come to room temperature again.

CHAPTER TEN

Beverages

Adventure begins in the glass! A huge variety of offerings will keep you sipping for excitement.

Homemade Coconut Milk

(unsweetened)

Versatile, natural and full of nutritious fat, it is worth the quick recipe time it takes to make homemade coconut milk!

4 cups hot water, not boiling

1-1/2 cups unsweetened shredded coconut (use 2 cups if you plan to make ice cream from the coconut milk)

Yields 4 cups.

1. Place coconut and hot water in a large bowl together for 30 minutes, stirring first so that all of the coconut is wet.
2. After 30 minutes, pour mixture into a high-powered blender and puree for 50 seconds.
3. Pour through a fine strainer and press on the solids to extract as much liquid and fat as possible.
4. Discard the pulp (or dehydrate it to make homemade coconut flour) and store the milk in the fridge for two to three days. The cream will separate and rise over time, so stir it back in according to your needs.

Variations:

- For a sweet treat, add 2 to 4 whole dates to Step 1, the hot soaking. Puree the dates into the milk, and the straining becomes optional. This is great to use for chia seed porridge, where the nubby texture and whole-food fiber are a bonus.
- Add 1/2 teaspoon vanilla or cinnamon to the blender before pureeing.

Creamy Warm Horchata Eggnog

(dairy-free, stevia-sweetened, nut-free option)

The vanilla bean is the fruit of the vanilla orchid flower. The whole fruit is dried, and while usually just the inside of the bean is scraped and used, if you have a high-powered blender, such as a Blendtec or VitaMix, the entire fruit can be pureed with great success. The bean's outer skin has a strong vanilla flavor and adds more vanilla essence to this lovely horchata. If you do not have a high-powered blender, scraping out the insides of the bean or using vanilla extract work great, too.

3-1/2 cups water

1 cup cashews or pine nuts, soaked and wet (see Appendix 2: Methods)

(or substitute 3 cups water + 1/4 cup chia seeds for a nut-free, no-soak version)

4 egg yolks, preferably grass-fed

2 tablespoons extra-virgin coconut oil

1 tablespoon sustainably sourced gelatin

1/2 an entire vanilla bean, or 1 teaspoon vanilla

1/2 teaspoon cinnamon

1/8 teaspoon powdered stevia + optional additional 1/16 teaspoon (or 15 to 20 drops liquid stevia — NuNaturals brand preferred)

Serves 6 to 8.

1. Place water in a high-powered blender. Add the soaked nuts, cinnamon, stevia and vanilla. Blend on medium-high speed for about 50 seconds. (For the nut-free, chia-seed option blend on medium-high speed for about 50 seconds.)
2. Pour approximately 1/3 of the milk mixture into a small to medium- size saucepan.
3. Sprinkle gelatin over the surface of the milk and, using your mixing spoon, push the gelatin under the surface of the foamy milk, allowing it to dissolve for 1 minute.
4. Heat pan over medium heat, stirring the milk, for approximately 3 minutes, until the milk is steaming hot but not yet simmering.
5. Pour this hot milk back into the cool milk that remains in the blender.
6. Add egg yolks and coconut oil.
7. Blend briefly to mix the ingredients and melt the oil, 10 to 15 seconds.
8. Serve the beverage warm, or chill to create a creamy custard that goes well with baked goods.

Variation:

- For a sweeter milk, add 1 to 2 tablespoons sweetener of choice: local raw honey, pure maple syrup or hardwood-derived xylitol.

Hot Chocolate

(dairy-free)

3 cups water

3/4 cup cashews or pine nuts

1/2 cup maple syrup, raw honey, hardwood-derived xylitol (Global Sweet brand recommended) or coconut sugar

1/3 cup cocoa

2 teaspoons sustainably sourced gelatin (optional)

1 teaspoon vanilla

1/8 teaspoon powdered stevia (or 15 drops liquid stevia — NuNaturals brand recommended)

1/8 teaspoon sea salt

Serves 3 to 4.

1. Place water in a blender and sprinkle its surface with the gelatin.
2. Add all of the remaining ingredients.
3. Blend the ingredients on medium-high speed for one full cycle, or about 1 minute.
4. Pour chocolate milk into a medium-size saucepan and stir over medium heat until hot and steamy but not yet simmering.
5. Serve.

Beet Kvass with Raspberries

This fermented beverage is easy to make, high in nutrition from the "super-food" beets, and is, of course, full of probiotics.

4 cups filtered water

1 large beet (about 1-1/2 to 2 cups, chopped into about 1-inch cubes, not grated or diced)

1/2 cup raspberries, fresh or frozen

1 tablespoon whey, strained from yogurt through a coffee filter or cheesecloth

1/16 teaspoon powdered stevia (or about 10 to 15 drops of liquid stevia — NuNaturals brand preferred)

Serves 4. Recipe doubles well.

1. Place beet pieces into a quart-size glass canning jar.
2. Add whey.
3. Fill jar to within 1 inch of the neck with filtered water.
4. Stir and cover, screwing the lid on loosely to allow gases to escape.
5. Keep the brew at room temperature and out of direct sunlight for two days in warm weather, or up to eight days or longer in colder weather.
6. After the kvass has deepened in color, has a pleasantly sour flavor, and shows signs of bubbles near the surface, or active effervescence, strain all but 1/4 cup from the glass jar into your serving or storage container.
7. To the strained kvass, add the raspberries and stevia. Stir and cover.
8. Transfer to the refrigerator. Chill and serve within one week.
9. For a future batch, add to the remaining beets 1/4 cup liquid, and fill this jar again with fresh filtered water. (Do not add new whey.)

10. Again, keep the mixture at room temperature for two to eight days minimum.

11. This second beverage may be milder and less potent than the first. The beets are now "exhausted" and can be thrown away; but 1/4 cup of the strained kvass may again be used for a following batch in place of whey.

Variations:

- Instead of using filtered water, strongly brewed hibiscus tea may be cooled and substituted.

- A 1-inch piece of fresh ginger or turmeric nub, chopped into four pieces, can be added before the fermentation process begins.

- 2 teaspoons lavender blossoms, 1 to 2 tablespoons citrus zest, 1 cinnamon stick, or 1/4 teaspoon cayenne may be added and fermented for flavor variations and nutrition, then strained out with the beets.

Stevia Lemonade

The stevia flavor is not as detectable amid the strong, wooing flavor of fresh lemon juice. The beverage is thirst-quenching and delicious alone, but it also makes a great liquid base for any smoothie.

8 cups water

1-1/2 cups lemon juice, preferably freshly squeezed

1/4 teaspoon powdered stevia (NuNaturals brand preferred)

Yields 9-½ cups

1. Stir to combine all ingredients using a whisk or long wooden spoon.

2. Chill and serve.

Tarragon or Basil Limeade with Honey

5 cups water

1 cup lime juice

3/4 cup honey

1 cup fresh tarragon, loosely packed (or 1-1/2 cups fresh basil)

1/2 cup water

Serves 6.

1. Combine the 5 cups water and honey in a medium-size saucepan over medium heat. Stir to dissolve the honey.
2. Allow the honey water to get very hot — steaming but not yet simmering.
3. Turn off the heat and add the tarragon or basil, steeping it for 30 minutes.
4. Strain out the fresh herbs by pouring the mixture through a mesh strainer into a large serving pitcher.
5. Add the lime juice and additional water. Stir well.
6. Chill and serve.

"Juiced Tea" — Marionberry Rooibos with Honey

This is one of my kids' and husband's favorite beverages. Often made for birthday parties or outdoor gatherings, it is also versatile, delicious made with a variety of teas and fruits.

4 cups strong rooibos tea, still warm but not hot

1 cup marionberries

1/2 cup honey

Serves 4.

1. Puree all the ingredients in a blender on medium speed for about 1 minute, until the berries are smooth and the honey is fully dissolved.
2. Strain through a mesh colander to remove seeds, and into a large serving pitcher.
3. Chill, stir and serve. Garnish with additional fresh, floating berries.

Honey-Spice Lassi

Lassis are functional as well as delicious. In Indian and Ayurvedic traditions they are used as digestives. Ginger, too, is prized for this property, helping our bodies to digest and assimilate nutrients with greater ease. There are two kinds of lassis served in India: savory and sweet — both made with thinned yogurt, which provides probiotics, potential grass-fed fat and protein. Ayurvedic wisdom does not condone cold drinks for digestion. So try drinking your lassi at room temperature or cool, but not cold.

2-1/2 cups yogurt, kefir or cream — all fully cultured

2 tablespoons raw honey (optional)

1 heaping tablespoon fresh ginger, freshly grated

1/8 teaspoon cinnamon

1/8 teaspoon freshly grated nutmeg, plus more for garnish

1/16 teaspoon powdered stevia (or 10 drops liquid stevia — NuNaturals brand preferred; if you omit the honey, increase the amount of stevia, to taste)

Serves 4 to 6.

1. Combine all of the ingredients in a blender and puree until completely mixed.
2. Serve in pretty glasses.
3. Garnish each portion with additional nutmeg.

Cardamom-Rose Water Lassi

2-1/2 cups yogurt, kefir or cream — all fully cultured

1 teaspoon pure rose water

1/8 teaspoon ground cardamom

1/16 to 1/8 teaspoon powdered stevia (or 10 to 15 drops liquid stevia — NuNaturals brand preferred)

Serves 4 to 6.

1. Combine all ingredients in a blender and puree until completely mixed.
2. Serve in pretty glasses.

Cilantro-Mint Lassi

(dairy-free)

2-1/2 cups warm water

1/2 cup dried unsweetened coconut

1 tablespoon fresh cilantro

2 leaves fresh mint

2 teaspoons fresh ginger, grated

1/2 teaspoon cumin, toasted briefly over medium heat in a pan until fragrant — about 30 seconds to 1 minute (omit for an AIP version)

1 to 2 grinds freshly ground black pepper

1/8 teaspoon sea salt

1/16 teaspoon powdered stevia (or 5 to 8 drops liquid stevia — NuNaturals brand preferred)

probiotics (a high quality capsule or 1/4 cup liquid from a home-fermented food, such as kvass, sauerkraut or water kefir; optional)

spirulina (or blue green algae) for garnish

Serves 4 to 6.

1. Combine water and coconut in a blender, and puree for 50 seconds.
2. Pour the puree through a fine strainer, pushing on the solids and catching the milk in a medium-size bowl.
3. Rinse out blender and transfer the homemade coconut milk back into it.

4. Add remaining ingredients to the blender and puree until the fresh herbs are teeny and the mixture is well combined — about 50 seconds on medium speed.
5. Serve in pretty glasses.
6. Garnish each portion with a small cilantro leaf and a sprinkling of spirulina.

Chia Electrolyte Beverage

We like to take this along in a water bottle whenever we have "marathon" events away from the house, such as long dance rehearsals or track events, or when we're fighting a bug and want to stay strong and hydrated.

4 cups filtered water

1/4 cup freshly squeezed lemon juice (or 2 tablespoons apple cider vinegar)

2 tablespoons chia seeds

1 tablespoon peeled fresh ginger, finely grated

1/4 teaspoon sea salt

1/8 teaspoon powdered stevia (or 10 to 15 drops liquid stevia — NuNaturals brand preferred)

1/8 teaspoon cayenne (optional)

Yields about 4 cups.

1. Combine all ingredients in a large pitcher or water bottle, stirring or shaking well to distribute the chia seeds so they do not clump together.
2. Allow a minimum of 10 minutes for the chia seeds to expand and become gel-like, stirring or shaking once or twice during that time.
3. Serve or chill.

Ginger-Honey Milkshake

(stevia-sweetened option)

When my doctor advised me to stay away from fruit, I was also able to start having honey and cream. I no longer have fruit smoothies, but I LOVE fresh ginger root. And based on what sells at our ice cream shops, most people do. It's a healing food that really hits the spot. There are two ways to make this milkshake: One is dairy-free for those who can have fruit. It's made with coconut cream, and it's what I make for my kids because my daughter can't have dairy. This milkshake is EASY and SO good, a nice combination for our busy lives. And raw honey is full of enzymes and nutrients. It ends up being a good-for-you quick treat! SOOO refreshing. If you can't have honey, no problem: Use the xylitol or stevia options instead!

1 full tray of ice cubes, about 10 to 12

6 ounces filtered water

3/4 cup grass-fed heavy cream (or coconut cream, or cultured cream —such as Nancy's brand sour cream, which is grass-fed, organic, lactose-free and full of probiotics)

1-inch nub of fresh ginger root (more or less, to taste)

2 tablespoons raw, local honey or hardwood-derived xylitol (Global Sweet brand recommended)

or

1/4 teaspoon powdered stevia* (or 20 drops liquid stevia — NuNaturals brand preferred)

Serves 3 to 4.

1. Place the ice cubes, water, ginger and honey into a high-powered blender.
2. Blend the contents on medium-high speed for about 1 minute, watching for the perfect, smooth, crushed-ice consistency.
3. Stop the motor. Add the cream.
4. Blend again briefly, just to mix the ingredients.
5. Serve. This is especially good on a hot day when you're thirsty!

*The stevia-sweetened version of this recipe will be icier.

feeding kids

CHAPTER ELEVEN

Feeding Kids

Easy, Fast Recipes
(Plus Tips and Tricks) for a Healing Diet

When you want your kids to eat bone broth soups and lots of gently cooked veggies and meat, it is helpful to have a simple homemade dessert to use as a "carrot." To my 6-year-old, I say, "If you eat all your spinach and eggs, you can have blueberry pie for dessert." That takes away the whole battle — and even the majority of the distasteful expressions — and speeds up the meal. To my older kids, I say something more along the lines of, "We just have soup for lunch, but I made a really yummy pudding for dessert." And I show it to them. I always then hear things like, "Pudding!" or "That's OK, Mom. Thanks for making pudding." It enlivens the meal and adds fun and excitement to the day to include regular treats with less-exciting savory meals.

Because the pH balance of our bellies is a concern,* many experts advise those on healing diets not to eat fruits with savory foods. Meats digest best at a certain pH, and fruits can be counterproductive, as they create the opposite pH in the belly. If this is the case with you and your family, the above motivations still work. You just might need to make treats without fruit. Or make them only with fruits like blueberries and lemons, which don't increase alkalinity and are appropriate to eat with savory foods.

Baking soda is a concern for the same reason: It lowers the pH of the belly. So while I appreciated muffins with soup — especially during my first years on a healing diet, when I was still craving more bread and sweets — I learned to avoid using baking soda in baked goods as much as possible. I have included many baking soda-free recipes for this reason. When I do consume baking soda (because sometimes you just want that yummy bread treat), I always make sure to take an extra naturopath-recommended Betaine HCl pill. Look into these with your doctor, too. They put the acid pH back into your belly and help all the digestive organs to secrete necessary digestive juices. (Many on healing diets take one of these pills with every meal, regardless of baking soda.)

Of course there are lots of grain-free meals that are exciting in and of themselves — dinners like Savory Cobbler, Lettuce Wrap Tacos, Zucchini Noodle Pasta or Spaghetti Squash

*Meats and vegetables require and produce an acidic environment in our stomachs to aid in their digestion. Conversely, fruit produces an alkaline or base environment for its digestion. Therefore, it is counter-productive, especially for those of us with digestive problems, to eat the foods together. Low-sugar fruits should be enjoyed with new relish as a snack between meals, or finished 30 minutes before the main meal. Fruits also have a quick transit time, meaning they should digest quickly. Eating them with meats slows down their transit time, which can cause them to ferment in our GI tract, not ideal for any of us.

Spaghetti. I am grateful to have kids who really appreciate these foods, but it has been a process. When we first removed sugar from our diets, for instance, it was hard for all of us. It helped that we continued to enjoy small amounts of honey, and that we allowed ourselves to say, "Yes, this is hard, but it won't last forever." We used those sugar-free times as an opportunity to learn to persevere without too much complaining. But, as I mentioned above, we ate more grain-free baked goods during the first two years to help us transition.

After being on a healing diet for four years, we actually eat fewer baked goods than we used to, because too many nuts or too much coconut flour, for instance, can compromise the healing process. So my goal with this book is not that you eat more baked goods, but that you have excellent recipes when you do bake, and also that your grain-free, sugar-free treats are better for you, easy to digest and full of nutrition. And if you "cheat" by eating a lot of baked goods, like we did, at least you'll have the most digestible recipes on hand and have the big picture in mind, gradually tapering back as you gain momentum and as your sugar cravings fade.

Assembling ice cream sandwiches and other shenanigans—family fun.

I have created several dessert recipes that are EASY, fast and sometimes even a little quirky. These provide the opportunity to make something quick when you have a sweet tooth or need a pick-me-up. Several of them are intentionally sweetened only with stevia so that they are no-sugar treats. If you prefer to substitute honey or another natural sweetener, many of the recipes are flexible and can adapt. Put 1/8 to 1/4 cup sweetener into the main mixture, for instance, not into a crust. Provided you keep some basic pantry and cold storage items on hand at all times (see Pantry section), you'll have an arsenal at your disposal to make quick, healthy treats.

Marionberry Panna Cotta

(dairy-free, egg-free)

3 cups frozen marionberries (or other berries)

2 cups coconut milk or room-temperature water

2 tablespoons sustainably sourced gelatin

a favorite herbal tea, loose bulk tea or a tea bag (rooibos is great, but feel free to find other fun subtle flavors that will complement the berries)

1/8 cup chia seeds (optional, for added texture and nutrition; omit for AIP version)

1/8 teaspoon powdered stevia (or 10 to 15 drops liquid stevia — NuNaturals brand preferred)

Serves 4 to 6.

1. Place coconut milk or water in a small saucepan.
2. Sprinkle gelatin over it and allow to dissolve for 1 minute.
3. Heat coconut milk or water over medium heat, stirring for 2 to 3 minutes, until steaming hot but not yet simmering.
4. Remove gelatin coconut milk or water from heat and add your favorite tea. Allow it to steep for 5 minutes.
5. Remove tea bag or strain out the bulk tea, squeezing or pressing on solids to extract flavor, and stir in the remaining ingredients: berries and seeds.
6. Distribute the panna cotta among separate serving bowls before it gels up. Note: If your berries are not frozen, the panna cotta may take up to 3 hours to gel — or longer if poured into a larger serving container. If you use frozen berries, the gelatin sets up almost immediately, creating an instant treat.
7. Refrigerate until ready to serve.

Variations:

- Granny Smith apples, diced, work well. Freeze the apples pieces if you want the panna cotta to gel quickly.

- Garnish with Whipped Coconut Cream (Page 184) or Vanilla Crème Fraiche (Page 179).

- If you have an extra nut crust in the freezer, panna cotta can become a more formal and impressive pie filling in just moments. Pour the panna cotta into your pre-made crust, and chill until it is set.

- Fold 1 cup lightly sweetened whipped cream, cultured cream or homemade yogurt into the panna cotta to make what the Brits call a "fool." No kid is fool enough to pass up that creamy, fruity mass! Top with fresh berries to make it super special.

- Layer the Berry Fool with leftover grain-free cookies, broken in pieces, to make an exciting parfait. See Parfait recipes later in this chapter for more parfait ideas.

- Add 2 tablespoons fresh lemon or lime juice for a zesty fresh flavor addition. Or add a full 1/4 cup fresh citrus juice with the addition of 2 tablespoons local, raw honey.

Cultured Gelatin Americana

As I write, this is one of my daily favorites. By eating or drinking this lovely "sludge" with your meal, you are getting the benefits of both gelatin and a probiotic. On a hot summer day, this treat is refreshing and perfectly healthy. A guilt-free jiggle. Kids love the texture and the variety of flavors that can surprise them. See all the variations below, and keep it fun! Without any additional flavoring, the taste and texture mimics a sweet cottage cheese.

3-1/2 cups filtered water

1 cup cultured sour cream (homemade or Nancy's brand preferred)

1 tablespoon + 1 teaspoon sustainably sourced gelatin

1/4 teaspoon powdered stevia (or 20 drops liquid stevia — NuNaturals brand preferred)

Serves 4.

1. Place 1 cup of the water in a small saucepan.
2. Sprinkle gelatin over its surface, allowing it to dissolve for 1 minute.
3. Heat water over medium heat, stirring for 2 to 3 minutes, until steaming hot but not yet simmering.
4. Remove from heat and add remaining 2-1/2 cups water.
5. Add stevia, and stir to incorporate.
6. Transfer gelatin water to a glass bowl with a lid, and place in the refrigerator for 3 hours, until set.
7. Add sour cream, and stir to mix. The gelatin will break up but will not fully incorporate with the cream, similar to soft curds.
8. Serve with meals for a creamy probiotic treat that's great for healing the gut.

Variations:

- Add your favorite tea bag to the hot gelatin water, allowing it to steep for 3 to 5 minutes before removing it and adding the additional water and stevia.

  Recommended gentle teas include ginger, vanilla rooibos, chamomile blends and lavender. Decaffeinated teas are fine in moderation, if organic.

- Add vanilla, peppermint oil, citrus oil, rose water or orange flower water to taste.

Colorful Gelatin Squares

Serve these colorful gelatin squares with sweetened kefir or crème fraiche — or by themselves.

Cucumber-Tarragon/Mint

2 cups water

1/2 cup cucumber, cubed

2 tablespoons tarragon or mint, fresh and loosely packed

2 tablespoons + 1 teaspoon sustainably sourced gelatin

1 tablespoon lemon juice, optional

1/8 teaspoon powdered stevia (or 8 drops liquid stevia — NuNaturals brand preferred)

Strawberry-Lime

1-3/4 cup water

1 cup strawberries

1 tablespoon lime juice

2 tablespoons local raw honey

2 tablespoons + 1 teaspoon sustainably sourced gelatin

1/8 teaspoon powdered stevia (or 8 drops liquid stevia — NuNaturals brand preferred)

Blueberry-Beet

1-1/2 cups water + 1/2 cup freshly pressed beet juice

1 cup blueberries

2 tablespoons local raw honey

2 tablespoons + 1 teaspoon sustainably sourced gelatin

1/8 teaspoon powdered stevia (or 8 drops liquid stevia — NuNaturals brand preferred)

Vanilla Rooibos

2 cups rooibos or vanilla rooibos tea

2 tablespoons sustainably sourced gelatin

1 teaspoon vanilla

1/8 teaspoon powdered stevia (or 8 drops liquid stevia — NuNaturals brand preferred)

Green Tea-Spirulina

2 cups decaffeinated green tea

2 tablespoons sustainably sourced gelatin

1 tablespoon local raw honey

1/4 teaspoon spirulina

1/8 teaspoon powdered stevia (or 8 drops liquid stevia — NuNaturals brand preferred)

Serves 2 to 4.

1. Place 1/2 cup room-temperature water or tea in a small saucepan.
2. Sprinkle the surface with the gelatin and allow it to dissolve for 1 minute.
3. Heat water over medium heat, stirring for 2 to 3 minutes, until steaming hot but not yet simmering.
4. Remove water from the heat and whisk in the remaining ingredients.
5. For flavors that include solids, such as fresh herbs or chopped produce, pour the mix into a blender and puree on medium-high speed for 30 to 50 seconds, until the puree is fully smooth.
6. Pour the flavored gelatin into a shallow casserole dish or pan to chill.
7. Transfer gelatin to the refrigerator and allow it to chill until fully firm and sliceable. Times will vary — usually about 3 hours.
8. Cut gelatin into preferred shapes and sizes and serve alone or with lightly sweetened cultured dairy — or in another playful and pretty way.

Variations:

- Experiment with your own colors and ingredients to make more fun flavors!

Pumpkin Spice Pudding

(dairy-free, egg-free, stevia-sweetened)

1 can (BPA-free) organic pumpkin (or 2 cups leftover cooked winter squash)

1 cup hemp milk, unsweetened and preferably homemade (see Page 189) (Substitute coconut milk for an AIP version)

2 tablespoons extra-virgin coconut oil

1 tablespoon sustainably sourced gelatin

1 teaspoon cinnamon

1/2 teaspoon ginger

1/16 to 1/8 teaspoon powdered stevia (or 8 to 15 drops liquid stevia — NuNaturals brand preferred)

Serves 4.

1. Place hemp milk in a small saucepan.
2. Sprinkle gelatin over it and allow to dissolve for 1 minute. (If the milk is frothy and preventing the gelatin from dissolving, whisk it into the milk.)
3. Heat milk over medium heat, stirring for 2 to 3 minutes, until steaming hot but not yet simmering.
4. Remove milk from heat and whisk in remaining ingredients: pumpkin, coconut oil, stevia and spices.
5. Pour custard into small, pretty cups, and chill until set and firm. Chilling time will depend on size — 2 to 3 hours minimum.
6. Serve.

Variation:

- Serve custard warm, as a beverage. It is healing to the gut and a creamy, cozy treat. My mom enjoys this recipe almost on a daily basis, as a warm beverage that is part "meal."

Rooibos Chia Chai Horchata

(dairy-free, stevia-sweetened)

3 cups rooibos chai tea, cold or room temperature

1/4 cup chia seeds

6 egg yolks, preferably grass-fed

1 teaspoon vanilla

1/2 teaspoon cinnamon

1/16 teaspoon sea salt (optional)

1/8 teaspoon powdered stevia (or 8 to 15 drops liquid stevia — NuNaturals brand preferred)

Serves 4.

1. Combine all ingredients in a high-powered blender on medium speed for 30 seconds.
2. Allow mixture to "set up," or thicken, for 10 minutes.
3. Serve cold. Or heat it slowly over low heat, stirring continually with a whisk, until the mixture is warm, not hot.

Chia Seed Porridge with Apples

(dairy-free, stevia-sweetened)

1. Make Rooibos Chia Chai Horchata recipe, above.
2. Add 1/2 large peeled Granny Smith apple, diced and raw, or sautéed or steamed.
3. Add 3 tablespoons chia seeds per serving (or 1-1/4 cups seeds to the overall batch, stirring as it thickens so the seeds don't clump together)
4. Eat cold or warm, as desired.

Chocolate-Cinnamon Chia Porridge, or "Aztec Chia Porridge"

(dairy-free, stevia-sweetened)

Heading out the door and need a quick, easy breakfast or snack? This recipe makes a single serving, but it can easily be multiplied. It whisks up quickly in your serving bowl, gives energy and protein, and is pleasing to eat!

1-1/2 cups hot water

1/4 cup chia seeds

1 egg, preferably grass-fed

2 tablespoons cocoa

1 teaspoon vanilla

1/4 teaspoon cinnamon

1/8 teaspoon sea salt

1/16 teaspoon powdered stevia (or 8 drops liquid stevia — NuNaturals brand preferred)

Serves 1.

1. Place egg in a small mixing or serving bowl and whisk it well.
2. Add hot water and whisk again.
3. Add remaining ingredients — except the chia seeds — and mix again.
4. Finally, add chia seeds and whisk them in completely.

5. Allow porridge to set up for 10 minutes.
6. Serve.

Variations:

- To make this as a cold pudding, use 1/2 cup hot water whisked with the cocoa to make the cocoa flavor "bloom"; omit just the egg white and use 1 cup cold water.

- If you want less caffeine, reduce the cocoa to 1 tablespoon.

Easy Almond Butter Ice Cream

(dairy-free)

3 cups water

2 whole eggs, preferably grass-fed

3/4 cup almond butter, sprouted and homemade

1/4 cup sweetener of choice: local raw honey, pure maple syrup or xylitol (Global Sweet brand recommended)

1 tablespoon vanilla

1/16 teaspoon powdered stevia (or 8 drops liquid stevia — NuNaturals brand preferred)

Serves 4.

1. Combine all ingredients in a blender and puree until smooth and homogenized.
2. Process in an ice cream maker according to manufacturer's instructions.
3. Serve and eat it all; it does not freeze well.

Crème Fraiche Parfaits

Parfaits are the easiest way to create something new and pretty from leftovers. Layering moist, rich ingredients with a leftover baked good and/or sprouted nuts makes sure-to-please comfort food. Here are several recipe combinations:

Tiramisu: Cold water extract coffee or strongly brewed coffee (decaf is fine), can be poured over layers of leftover Chocolate Cake (Page 118), layered with sweetened Vanilla and Chocolate Crème Fraiche (Pages 176 and 179), and topped with shaved unsweetened chocolate, cocoa nibs or Lily's stevia-sweetened chocolate chips.

Berry Shortcake: Leftover berry muffins or scones (Pages 33, 35, 37, 46, 52) can be broken into chunks and layered with Berry Compote (Page 199) or fresh berries, and Vanilla Crème Fraiche (Page 179).

Neapolitan: Layer fresh or macerated strawberries (strawberries stirred with a small amount of water and honey or stevia) with leftover Chocolate Cake (Pages 118), Chocolate Crème Fraiche (Page 176) and Vanilla Crème Fraiche (Page 179).

Feeding Kids · 245

Top any parfait with fresh whipped cream when you serve, if cream is tolerated — or try Coconut Whipped Cream (Page 184).

Clafouti Parfaits

Use leftover Berry Clafouti (Page 138), cake or muffin. Layer cubes of leftover clafouti with any favorite creamy topping — sweetened Vanilla Crème Fraiche (Page 179), nut or seed custard (Page 188) or homemade fully cultured yogurt (Page 182); add nuts, fresh fruit or Berry Compote (Page 199) as additional layers. Allow parfaits 3 or more hours in the refrigerator so their flavors and texture set up; or serve immediately if you need a pretty treat in a hurry.

Dairy-Free Parfaits

Layer your favorite nut, seed or coconut-based Custard, Pudding or Porridge with fresh fruit, Berry Compote (Page 199), Sprouted Crispy Nuts (Page 270) or dried, unsweetened coconut, leftover cookies or baked goods, broken into chunks, and optional Coconut Whipped Cream (Page 184).

Egg-Free and/or Dairy-Free Parfaits

Nut crusts make a wonderful crumble. Layered with fruit and something rich and creamy, they'll make sure you won't miss the eggs. You can bake the crust ingredients in a preheated 375-degree-Fahrenheit oven, spread out in clumps on a baking sheet, until the nuts are fragrant, or use the crust crumble straight from the blender for a softer, milder effect.

- Use a preferred nut or seed crust recipe (see Pages 92, 95, 97, 99, 102, 104, 106) to layer with berries or Berry Compote (Page 199) and favorite creamy topping: homemade Fully Cultured Raw Yogurt (Page 182), Crème Fraiche (Page 179), Egg-Free Toppings (Pages 124, 184, 206, 210).

CHAPTER TWELVE

Foods NOT to Eat (and Why)

This list is not exhaustive, but I hope it will be helpful as a guide for either cleaning out your fridge, medicine cabinet and pantry or making new purchases in these categories.

*Monounsaturated canola oil and polyunsaturated vegetable oils
such as sunflower, soy, corn and safflower*

Historically, the oil from the rapeseed plant (now commonly known as canola) was used in Asian countries. Likely extracted at low heat, it was probably a healthful oil, not yet changed molecularly, and high in omega-3s. These days, the American seed has been modified and is extracted using high heat and solvents. The product is also bleached, degummed and refined at high temperatures. Trans-fats are created in a final process of deodorizing burned omega-3s. So while canola oil contains omega-3s, they are rancid and cancer-causing.

Regarding sunflower, safflower, corn and soy, these polyunsaturated oils are highly reactive by nature, forming free radicals when they are subjected to heat or oxygen — such as occurs during processing, extraction and cooking. Free radicals have been implicated in causing cancer and heart disease. These oils are high in omega-6s, which are already over-consumed by most Americans. This factor has been implicated in adult-onset diabetes, as well as other health problems. If you eat these oils, they should be produced by a company like Spectrum Organics and be expeller-pressed. They should not be heated at all and should be eaten in great moderation.

White refined sugar and corn syrup

Refined sugar has no nutrients at all; they are removed during the refinement process. The body is forced to draw on its own storage of vitamins, minerals and enzymes to correct an imbalance that occurs when sugar is consumed. Eating nutrient-void foods also creates an over-acid condition that overtaxes the body as it seeks to correct the problem. Dental decay, diabetes, gallstones, hypoglycemia, mental issues, addiction, adrenal fatigue, obesity and pathogen overgrowth are but a few of the known issues related to consumption or over-consumption of refined sweeteners.

One other issue is genetic modification, which I discuss below. Corn syrup, if not organic, is genetically modified. Other refined sugars are also heading that direction, as countries like Egypt try to increase their output following the mono-crop model. Nature cannot support such unreasonable volumes, which are detrimental to the land and its ecosystem.

Most packaged and processed foods contain sugar and/or corn syrup. They may be convenient, but at what cost? Our bodies deserve whole foods. Learn a few new recipes (such as grain-free, sugar-free bars and muffins that can travel and that freeze well) and ditch the packaged convenience foods!

Agave nectar

This newly created sweetener, developed during the 1990s, is not as natural, diabetic-safe and raw as it is advertised to be. It is highly refined and has a profile similar to high-fructose corn syrup. The fructose contained in it is dangerous in terms of the many conditions it can cause: insulin resistance, mineral depletion, liver inflammation, high blood pressure, heart disease and more. Surprisingly, all brands of agave nectar have more fructose than corn syrup. It also has high levels of saponin, which can cause miscarriage.

Dry cereal, even granola

A high-heat process used to make all dry cereals renders them completely void of nutrients, or in some cases sorely lacking them — even organic breakfast cereals. A wonderfully insightful and shocking test done on rats showed that they could survive longer on cardboard than on cereal. Cereal is fortified with vitamins and minerals, but there is NO food value in the cereal itself. Many of us like the texture, sugar and experience of eating a bowl of cereal or granola. We are well-advised to change our habits. There are so many good alternatives: hot cereal, eggs, homemade sprouted granola and nuts, winter squash "porridge," sourdough or sprouted or grain-free baked goods, fresh fruit or veggies for a crunchy snack, yogurt, aged cheese or frozen yogurt for dessert, etc.

Multivitamins

Of course, this decision is very personal, and I am not a nutritionist or a doctor, nor do I pretend to be one. My beliefs are based on the reading I've done and the thinkers I agree with. In a nutshell, here is something that GAPS physician Dr. Natasha Campbell-McBride shares on this subject that I think is worthy of consideration: "I am very careful with multi-vitamin, mineral and amino acid supplements. With the majority of patients, I don't give it at all. I just tell them to implement the diet [Nourishing Traditions or GAPS, if needed] fully. Once the diet is fully implemented, the nutritional deficiencies just go away because the body knows what to do with vitamins, minerals, and amino acids when they come as food. When they come as supplements the majority are synthetic. They don't come with the right kind of co-factors, the right kind of friends holding hands, so the body doesn't recognize them. And for most of the common supplements on the market today, the absorption rate is very low."

I have read that the average absorption rate is 9 percent for most vitamins. If you believe that a vitamin supplement is an important part of your health, I agree that supplementation in certain cases is essential to restore optimum health. A trustworthy doctor/naturopath knows which brands are effective and how to keep your body balanced. We must use educated caution when introducing pills. They must all be in balance with one another. If your health situation does not need intervention, enjoy juicing and eating lots of different (raw) vegetables and organ meats. (Those with leaky gut need to exercise care to rotate the vegetables juiced, so as not to create new food allergies. Waiting four days to repeat a food is a good rule when rotating.) Minerals in liquid form, such as soil minerals, can also be a good option for those who do need intervention for healing.

> *Additionally, it is helpful to know if you have the MTHFR gene mutation. Recently gaining more visibility, this gene mutation affects many of us with health challenges. Proper B Vitamin supplementation is required to help the body to detoxify and to heal. Dr. Ben Lynch is a leading educator on this topic. See his website and recommendations for greater insight, as well as discussing this with your doctor. His many tips include making sure the supplements you do take include folate instead of folic acid.*

The nutritionists I've read HIGHLY recommend, however, supplementing our diets with a fermented cod liver oil/butter. This can come in pill form (Blue Ice Royal by Green Pasture), for those who can't tolerate the flavor.

In summation, most vitamins are synthetic and are not in a biochemical form to be recognized and absorbed. They are made cheaply and tax our bodies to quickly excrete them as waste. However, there may be some supplementation required for healing. These options should be discussed, ideally with a functional practitioner. (Of special consideration is the issue of folic acid. It is synthetic and should be replaced by folate. Ask your doctor and check your supplements. Folic acid, while once recommended for pregnant women and found in most multi-vitamins, is now being implicated as cancer-causing and dangerous.)"

Conventional, genetically modified crops

Genetic modification is a relatively new form of human naiveté and pride in our own knowledge. Believing we can improve on the Earth's design, we have changed the genetic package that is a plant to take away or give certain attributes we think will make our lives more convenient. Time and again, our own "progress" of this kind in recent history has led to major trouble. (The overuse of antibiotics is another example of human ingenuity causing a detriment to nature and our optimum health.)

The following conventional crops are always genetically modified in our current world. It is best to find these foods organic or in some of the cases (such as canola) to avoid them altogether: soy, corn, cottonseed, canola, sugar from sugar beets, Hawaiian papaya, zucchini and crookneck squash. Many other conventional crops are also subject to genetic modification, of course, as well. Organic, local produce is the best choice to make you feel good, to benefit your body and to stop the power of major agricultural companies that cause worldwide damage in their blind sweep of this fragile ecosystem.

Chlorinated water

Chlorine was discovered, and then harnessed, to kill. It was first used as a weapon of war. It has saved millions of lives in areas where extreme sanitation needs to take place. But in our daily lives, it has no place. It kills; therefore we should not drink it! At the very least, buy a good-quality filtered water pitcher to protect your body if your city water is chlorinated. Also see the Resources page in this book (Page 267) for recommended water filters.

Unfermented soy

There are four forms of fermented soy that are safe to consume: fermented soy sauce, tempeh, miso and natto. All other forms of soy are hormone-altering. Soy inhibits the digestion of protein and is linked with cancer in many different studies. Unfermented soy also impairs thyroid and immune system functions.

Conventional dairy and skim and low-fat milk

Conventional dairy is almost always genetically modified. Also, feedlot cattle, which are fed corn and soy, produce meat and milk that has 20 times the omega-6 ratio to that of grass-fed animals. (Remember, Americans already consume too many omega-6s.) This is the beef and dairy fat that causes heart disease. Meanwhile, grass-fed meat and milk products are comparable to heart-healthy wild salmon in their fatty acid profile — the right balance of omega-3s to omega-6s.

The vitamins found in milk are fat-soluble; they require fat to be absorbed and utilized by the body. Consuming nonfat and low-fat dairy products interferes with the ability to benefit from these naturally occurring vitamins.

Nonfat and low-fat milks have been denatured or altered during high-heat pasteurization, which makes them more harmful than healthful.

Fat-free milk is fed to conventional pigs leading up to slaughter as a means of fattening them up; it signals the body that something is missing, which leads to overeating. Therefore, fat-free diets do not help us to lose weight or keep our weight down. Low-sugar diets do this. High-fat diets help to satisfy us, in addition to providing necessary nutrients.

Protein powder

I'm going to quote an expert because he says it so succinctly. Tim Boyd, a writer and researcher from the Weston A. Price Foundation, writes that protein powders "usually contain carcinogens formed during processing; and consumption of protein without the cofactors occurring in nature can lead to deficiencies, especially of vitamin A." If we need quick protein, we should find a whole food that can do the trick.

Aluminum-containing foods

Products such as baking powder, traditional table salt and antacids contain aluminum, as do many processed foods, certain deodorants and cosmetics. Aluminum has been linked to brain diseases such as Alzheimer's. Aluminum affects the musculoskeletal system, as well, thwarting the growth of muscles and bones, and hindering development in children. Dementia, seizures and overall mental function can be caused by a build-up of aluminum. Also avoid processed cheeses (one more reason!) and pickles that contain aluminum.

CHAPTER THIRTEEN

Glossary of Ingredients

Through friends, relatives, customers and cooking-class participants, I have discovered that we all have different thresholds for how much we want to know about nutrition and food. We can only take in so much! And when we're changing our diets, the learning curve can be very steep. My approach is: "Do what you can, and don't let yourself feel guilty for what you can't take on." Baby steps are great. Sometimes small, slow steps are more thorough, better-embraced steps. And then, once mastered, we are ready for the next piece of information or new ingredient. This book uses that approach. Here in the glossary, I have provided both "macro" definitions (**bold print**) and "micro" definitions for each ingredient. If you are hungry to learn more, read the whole entry. If you just want an introduction to an ingredient, read only the "macro" definition. *Voila!* I've just made it easier (I hope) for you to take this journey at your own pace!

Almonds and Almond Products. Most conventional almonds undergo a gassing process. Propylene oxide gas, a "probable" carcinogen, is often used to pasteurize almonds, as a result of 2007 legislation. No U.S. grown almonds are raw. Bagged almond meal, or blanched almond flour, has therefore been compromised significantly; it likely contains residues that are cancer-causing. Additionally, the almond crop puts an undue strain on the state of California during a drought. The crop requires copious amounts of water and is not sustainable. Thirdly, all nuts have a short shelf life. They are prone toward rancidity. All commercially made almond butter, almond meal, almond flour, and blanched almond flour is likely rancid and best to avoid. We must also consider that most commercially made almond products are not sprouted; so they are hard to digest and wreak havoc on our digestive mechanisms. The final consideration when consuming almonds, assuming they are fresh and sprouted and ideally not from California (Italy is a popular source for organic, raw almonds) is their omega-6 profile. Almond's omega-6 to omega-3 ratio is heavy on the omega-6 side. The typical American diet is already heavy in omega-6's, which is why so many doctors now recommend foods and supplementary fish oils high in omega-3's, to get the balance back to where it should be. In conclusion, I recommend eating almonds only occasionally. I do not think they are a good everyday staple food. When we do eat them they need to be fresh and sprouted.

Bee pollen. **Resembling dusty, mustard-colored pellets, bee pollen adds a subtle grainy texture to smoothies. Used as an energy booster and to increase endurance, bee pollen is very high in vitamins C and B. It is considered a super food because of its high amino acid profile, which makes it also high in protein.** Bee pollen is a great add-in for free amino acids (meaning highly usable protein and super food nutrition). It is higher in vitamins than any other single food. Shown to promote longevity and energy, it contains especially beneficial enzymes, along with minerals such as iron, calcium, magnesium and zinc. **However, if you have asthma or seasonal allergies, use bee pollen with caution.** It can trigger an allergic response in some sensitive individuals.

Blue-green algae. (See Spirulina.)

Bone broth. **This soothing elixir contains minerals and amino acids that the body needs to heal itself. A leaky or damaged gut can be transformed through the consumption of bone broth and soups that are built around it.** Sustainably sourced bones can range in price from free or $1 a pound if bought in bulk up to $4 per pound. About 1-1/2 pounds of bones are used for each batch of broth that fills a slow cooker. So it's a very economical super food. Check out "How to Make Bone Broth" on my blog, www.eatbeautiful.net, to see the full recipe for perfect bone broth. The minerals from bone broth are easy for the body to assimilate and actually aid in digestion. Also, if made in a slow cooker, bone broth is actually a "fast food." Once assembled, it takes care of itself and is easy to consume as needed.

Butter. Full of healthy saturated fat — and, to a lesser degree, healthful monounsaturated fats — butter is considered a true health food by proponents such as the Weston A. Price Foundation. **Its low smoke point makes it ideal only for low-medium temperature cooking or baking — unlike its counterpart, ghee, which can tolerate higher-heat applications. Butter contains antioxidant properties and helps provide healthy cholesterol. Vitamins A, D, E and K, — and lecithin, too — are found in high amounts in butter, aiding in adrenal and thyroid function, as well as in cardiovascular health. Grass-fed butter in particular is butter that comes from cows that graze on grass instead of consuming grain. Their cream is substantially higher in omega-3s and beta carotene. And, contrary to modern false information promoted by the FDA, butter from grass-fed cows actually helps to prevent heart disease. It is especially high in vitamins A and E, as well as the mineral selenium. Recent articles in mainstream news sources such as** *The Wall Street Journal* **and** *TIME* **magazine have finally begun to inform consumers regarding the truth about butter.**

Chia seeds. **Advocates of these tiny seeds, which are high in omega-3s, claim they pack a powerful energy punch. Chia seeds do not require pre-soaking or sprouting, and they are easily digested. When added to liquid, the seeds gel, creating a convenient egg substitute for use in baked goods, as well as a healthy way to make instant puddings, porridges and electrolyte beverages.**

Organic cocoa (not Dutch process). **No chemicals are used in this kind of cocoa. It is pure cacao beans — an unprocessed, whole food.** Cocoa, when handled properly, is also carefully fermented. (Dutch process cocoa is chemically treated and refined; it doesn't taste anything like quality organic cocoa, and it is potentially harmful to people and the planet.)

Coconut flour. Several commercial brands of coconut flour are now available. It can also be homemade, as a byproduct of making coconut milk. (Simply dehydrate the leftover fiber after the milk is strained and pressed from it. Then blend the dried fiber into flour in your blender or spice grinder.) **Commercial brands are functional rather than**

nutritious. They have been processed at high heat, and some people who are allergic to coconut can tolerate them because they have so little left in them that is actually coconut! The flour is just fiber that helps to create a certain texture in baked goods. That is why I like to use the ingredient sparingly. It is a great tool for texture, but it adds little to nothing nutritionally. Homemade coconut flour has more nutrition and **coconut essence.** However, I am not a snob about only making and using homemade. The convenience of buying commercially made coconut flour is an acceptable crutch. We all need the occasional easy go-to. And not much of it is used in my recipes — just a little to create the right effect. **One other benefit of coconut flour is that it does not contain phytates** (acids that interfere with the absorption of nutrients), which are found in nuts and seeds. So if you need to limit your nut and seed consumption to protect the amount of minerals you are absorbing (see Sprouted Nuts and Seeds below), coconut flour can be a good substitution. However, too much fiber can be, well, too much — contrary to modern advice from many doctors. So limit your coconut flour ingestion as well. All things in moderation, right?

Coconut milk. The liquid in the center of a coconut is not coconut milk. Rather, coconut milk comes from pureeing the meat of the coconut with water and then straining the solids out. It's naturally sweet, creamy and high in "good" fats. For higher fat, homemade coconut milk increase the ratio of dried coconut to water, and vice versa. If you have the time to make it, coconut milk is lovely homemade and is a nice way to avoid canned foods that usually contain guar gum and sometimes a BPA liner. (See recipe on Page 214.)

Coconut oil. Coconut oil is extracted from the meat or "kernel" of the coconut. It is ideal to buy extra-virgin coconut oil, as refined coconut oil has been processed with chemicals — and often with bleach and pesticides, too, if not organic. Extra-virgin and expeller-pressed designations on the label help ensure quality and healthfulness. You will still find certain brands that are fresher than others. **Coconut oil, a saturated fat, is very stable and can be used for medium-heat to high-heat cooking. Consumed raw, it has many health benefits.**

Coconut sugar. This is a natural sugar derived from the sap of the coconut palm tree. It is lower on the glycemic index than sugar but still contains moderately high levels of fructose and should be consumed in moderation.

Dates. These are the fruit of the date palm. **The dates we buy in the United States are usually dried, and are therefore a source of concentrated fruit sugar. Because dates are sweeter than any other dried fruit (their closest competitors are bananas and raisins), they make an excellent natural sweetener.** Pureeing dates into batters is one of my favorite techniques, as they also add an extra-nice touch of texture to baked goods. **Exercise caution when consuming dates if you are sugar-sensitive — especially, for instance, if you are fighting pathogen overgrowth.**

Duck fat (and other animal fats rendered from grass-fed animals). We need not question whether animal fats of any kind are healthy. Nature knows what it's doing. If an animal is raised eating what it should eat (and is not being fed what's cheapest or produces the most meat quickly), its meat and fat will be healthful. **Duck fat has become trendier in our country lately, but nothing has changed. Saturated fats are stable and safe for medium- and high-heat cooking, and are actually easy for the body to recognize and digest.** The fat profile of duck fat is great: It's largely monounsaturated, with some saturated fat, and very little polyunsaturated fat. Brain health and general energy are produced largely from good quality fats. As you may already know, fat doesn't get stored as fat in our body; that's what happens with sugar! Good fats are just plain good for us.

Extra-virgin olive oil. This oil is pure and natural, pressed easily from olives, and is stable and safe to cook or bake with up to medium temperatures. You do want to balance your consumption of olive oil with saturated fats, as your body needs more than the monounsaturated fat that olive oil provides. Olive oil is a great source of antioxidants. Do not buy olive oil blends, such as "lite" olive oil or regular olive oil. Buy only extra-virgin.

Flaxseeds. These are easy to digest, but the fat must be converted in our bodies into omega-3s, making it an inefficient way of getting the right fats in our diet. Still, these seeds are a good choice occasionally — just not exclusively or too often. There are better sources for regular intake of "good fats." Flaxseeds are also noteworthy for the role they play in baking. Like chia seeds, they have a binding quality that can be a helpful substitute for eggs in baked goods, where they also add to moistness.

Gelatin. Gelatin is a melted form of collagen. The proteins are soluble in hot water. Common sources for gelatin are cowhide and pig skin. Great Lakes brand offers a more sustainably sourced gelatin than was available until recently. I have also discovered and enjoyed using the Vital Proteins brand. **Gelatin and collagen are helpful in rebuilding the gut lining. Gelatin provides amino acids that not only help to repair the gut, but also aid healing in various areas of the body, including the skin, heart, bone, muscle, cartilage and immune system. Gelatin is additionally beneficial because it is gentle and easy to digest. Often those who cannot tolerate most foods can still easily digest and utilize gelatin dissolved in water, or gelatin-rich bone broth.** Gelatin also aids in the digestion of milk, milk products and milk fat. Gelatin helps to normalize the pH of the stomach, too, aiding in general digestion and helping the digestive organs to secrete necessary digestive juices. Conditions such as rheumatoid arthritis and irritable bowel syndrome have shown measurable improvement when gelatin is included in the diet.

Ghee. This is "clarified butter" — butter that has been heated and simmered to separate out the casein, whey and lactose so that they can be skimmed off. Therefore, ghee is much more allergy-friendly than butter for those on healing diets. **An added benefit is that ghee can be used for high-heat cooking because it is stable and has a high smoke point. Ghee also does not need to be refrigerated.** Some of the nutrients in butter are even more highly concentrated in ghee, making it a healthy fat, indeed.

Goji berries. This fruit — high in protein and trace minerals and low in certain sugars — is touted as a super food. Caution is advised, however, for those who are sensitive to

foods that belong to the nightshade family, those on medication for diabetes or high blood pressure, as well as those who take blood thinners. Goji berries are also celebrated for being high in antioxidants and having immune-boosting properties. For the purposes of a healing diet, it is noteworthy that goji berries are high in polysaccharides — sugars that provides longer-term energy, because they are digested by the body more slowly than simple sugars like glucose.

Guar gum. **Often found in canned coconut milk, this ingredient is not a whole food but is included in many processed foods to affect the texture or stability of the product.** Guar gum is derived from the seeds of the guar bean, mostly grown in India and Pakistan, where the whole beans are actually eaten regularly. **Guar gum can cause GI discomfort in sensitive individuals.** Listen to your body and be aware of the potential. Avoid most canned coconut milks if you notice any symptoms. (To make your own milk, see Page 214.)

Hemp seeds. Easy to digest, hemp seeds have an ideal omega-3 to omega-6 ratio, and they are high in protein with a full amino acid profile. Conveniently, hemp seeds don't require soaking and sprouting. They are naturally gentle and easy to digest.

Going clockwise from top left: hemp seeds, chia seeds, bee pollen, spirulina, hibiscus (bottom left), elderberries (center) and goji berries (in righthand corners).

Glossary of Ingredients · 261

Hibiscus. **Hibiscus petals are astringent, citrusy and fruity. They are also valued for high levels of vitamin C, balancing blood pressure levels and for fighting inflammation.** Many cultures help treat diabetes and insomnia with hibiscus. Tea from the flowers is broadly enjoyed internationally, and often medicinally.

Lard. **This refers to the fat rendered from pigs.** The profile of pork fat reveals that the greatest part is monounsaturated, with slightly less saturated fat, and very little polyunsaturated fat. Lard is also high in vitamin D. (For more information on the benefits of animal fats, see "Duck fat.")

Lavender. **Lavender blossoms are a culinary gem, a wonderful herb in French savory cooking, often paired with thyme and rosemary to flavor roasted chicken. Reputed for its calming effect, dried lavender has gained new popularity more recently in cookies, custard, ice cream and tea blend recipes.** Steeping lavender for 10 minutes in hot milk, cream, or coconut milk (then straining) creates a lovely base for creamy desserts. Use 2 tablespoons of the bulk dried flowers for every 3 cups milk or cream.

Local. **When used to describe food, this term means that what you consume is grown or raised within 100 miles of where you live.**

Local raw honey. **High in minerals and considered a whole food, honey is used as a sweetener in GAPS, Paleo and other sugar-free diets.** It is not technically considered vegan because it comes from animals. Ancient Ayurvedic medicine does not recommend heating honey or cooking with it. However, the Weston A. Price Foundation does not substantiate this. Substitute other sweeteners in baked goods if it is a concern for you. I appreciate an excerpt from an article written for the WAPF by Jen Allbritton, who says, "Our ancestors likely indulged in around one tablespoon … of honey per day (when available), which is stunningly low compared to today's average sugar intake of one cup … per day!" This insight puts our treats into perspective. **Honey is truly a healthy sugar alternative, but all sweets should be eaten in moderation and with lots of good fat at the same time! The fat helps the body digest the sugar more slowly, keeping all systems in balance.**

Pure maple syrup. **A sweetener that is refined very little, pure maple syrup is a "whole food." Therefore, it is an acceptable sweetener for people who avoid sugar and pursue a whole-foods diet. It is high in trace minerals.**

Rose bud blossoms. **Dried rose petals are enjoyed globally and medicinally, made into tea, and rank high for their antioxidant levels. Rose petals help to heal and stimulate the digestive tract. They can improve symptoms of constipation, insomnia and depression. Emotionally, rose is known to be soothing. For women's health, rose has a reputation for balancing hormones and hormone-related symptoms.** A very small amount of caffeine is found in rose petals which *gently* stimulates the central nervous system.

One of my favorite photographs in this book: our three children and flowers.

Sauerkraut/fermented veggies. **Fermented veggies are vegetables that are allowed to ferment in a salt brine — sometimes inoculated with dairy whey — so that they might become a superfood with probiotics. These veggies are excellent for the immune system and for maintaining a balance of flora in the gut.** Fermented vegetables or other fermented foods (such as fully cultured yogurt), introduced slowly into the diet and eaten at every meal, are a great way to combat pathogen overgrowth.

Sesame seeds, hulled. **It's important to buy only hulled sesame seeds, so that your body will be able to digest them. The outer husk of sesame seeds is difficult to digest and renders the seed's nutrients inaccessible — not to mention it taxes the digestive mechanism.** I used to think anything that was "stripped" was less nutrient-dense. On the contrary, a hulled sesame seed is, in a sense, predigested. However, even hulled sesame seeds are high in phytates, so we should eat them in moderation.

Sprouted nuts and seeds. **Soaking nuts and seeds improves digestibility and nutrition and protects against overuse of our digestive system and disease. Soaking is not necessary with flaxseeds, chia seeds, hulled sesame seeds or hemp seeds.** Soaked nuts and seeds can be used in their soaked, wet state for baking and for making fermented vegan cheeses. Or they can be dehydrated for snacking or baking. Flour can be made from soaked and dehydrated nuts or seeds. **Once nuts or seeds have undergone this process, we say they are "sprouted." Though you might not see a sprout, enzymatically, the nut or seed has "awakened" from a dormant state.** Phytates are broken down during the soaking and sprouting process and continue to diminish during dehydrating and gentle roasting. Phytates are found in many foods, but especially in grains, nuts and seeds. Remember, they bind with minerals during digestion and therefore limit the amount of good nutrition we can access from our food.

Spirulina. **Considered a superfood, spirulina is an algae appreciated for its high protein and mineral content. It helps to balance blood sugar and is a good source of potassium and magnesium, which help with energy levels.** Sally Fallon, author of *Nourishing Traditions*, says spirulina is "rich in chlorophyll, protein, beta carotene, omega-3 fatty acids, … enzymes and nucleic acids … spirulina is said to be the easiest (dried algae) to digest and absorb." **People with hypothyroidism or serious seafood allergies should avoid this food.**

How do you sprout nuts and seeds? See the Methods section in Appendix 2 on Page 270.

Stevia. This is a plant that any of us could easily grow in our gardens. There are three main ways to enjoy and experiment with this natural sweetener: as an alcohol or glycerin-based tincture, as a white powder that is usually maltodextrin-based (corn derived), and as an actual green leaf in powdered or crushed form. **The tincture and the white powder are the most palatable forms, depending on the brand. I find that NuNaturals produces the best-tasting stevia, without a bitter or strong licorice flavor. NuNaturals has also created a white powder product without maltodextrin that is 99 percent pure stevia. If you do not use NuNaturals brand stevia in executing the recipes in this book, be aware that the strength of sweetness can vary considerably from brand to brand.** I have one glycerin-based tincture that requires only two drops to sweeten a 12-ounce cup of tea, whereas with NuNaturals alcohol-based tincture five to eight drops is used. Finally, if you have a negative perception of stevia, I would urge you to reconsider it. When used sparingly and from a good source, it is an amazing gift from nature. It cannot be substituted 1:1 for sugar or honey in baking or ice cream recipes because the texture and flavor will be altered. But I have formulated so many of my recipes for its use. It's like free sweetness. Receive the gift and cultivate an appreciation.

As you see in this cookbook, often I use stevia in conjunction with one other sweetener in a recipe. I have sometimes been asked why both sweeteners are needed. I use stevia with honey, for instance, to reduce the overall amount of fructose and glucose in a recipe or so the honey flavor will not dominate. I want the recipe to have a certain degree of sweetness, but if the texture of the finished product will not be affected I use some stevia to achieve this level.

Xanthan gum. This product is usually derived from genetically modified corn. However, you can find it made from organic, nongenetically modified corn. It helps the texture of certain products to be very smooth, mouth-feel-wise — especially nonfat and low-fat products. It can also suspend ingredients, helping to maintain texture or body in a baked good or beverage, preventing separation from occurring. The amount that goes into any recipe is teeny. It is not a whole food.

Xylitol. Most xylitol, in my experience, is better left on the grocery market shelves. Global Sweet (see Resources) is one of the only brands I've found that is derived from North American-grown hardwood. Some competitors (who make false claims about their ingredients) manufacture this alcohol sugar from corn grown in China, and the product then causes gastric distress for many. A product that produces any gas at all is taxing to our GI system. When xylitol is hardwood-derived, it has many noteworthy qualities. Most importantly, it isn't processed like sugar in the body, so unlike other natural sugar substitutes (except stevia) **it is low on the glycemic index and safe not only for diabetics but also for those of us on anti-candida, anti-inflammatory and other healing diets.** Xylitol is a polyol, a classification of molecules found in food that cause irritable bowel syndrome symptoms in some sensitive individuals. **So if xylitol doesn't agree with you, stick with other sweeteners.** You may heal from your sensitivity by staying away from the offending food. Xylitol is actually a prebiotic, so it can be too much too soon in a gut that does not have a healthy probiotic colony. Xylitol is additionally controversial because it isn't a whole food. We are well-advised to use it with caution and moderation. The reason I use it in this book is that I have seen it help many customers and recipe-consulting clients overcome sugar addiction and candida overgrowth.

APPENDIX 1

Recommended Sources for Food and Equipment

Blender	• Price-comparison shopping is recommended, but I like Blendtec's Wild Side model for the smoothest nut milks. And I like Fleetwood brand for its powerful commercial motor and its stainless steel jar — no plastic touches the food.
Sea salt	• A local, natural-food store • Online at Mountain Rose Herbs
Coconut oil	• A local, natural-food store • Online at Tropical Traditions or Amazon.com
Cricket flour	• Online at http://store.nextmillenniumfarms.com/category-s/1832.htm
Dehydrator	• Ultimate Nourishment's website has basic and all stainless steel models, some with approachable price points. I stay away from plastic appliances whenever I can.
Duck fat	• A local, gourmet meat market • A local poultry farmer, if grass-fed and sustainably raised (see Eatwild.com to find a farm near you) • Online from U.S. Wellness Meats

Extra-virgin olive oil	• When ordering online see Tropical Traditions and Olea Estates. • A local natural-food market, Costco or Trader Joe's, for the best price • Beware that some imported olive oils are not pure; use shopping discretion.
Food processor	• This item can be hard to shop for. My super fancy Cuisinart is difficult to clean. Choose the size "bowl" you want, and select the blades with care as well, making sure the machine does exactly what you want it to do and that there aren't too many nooks that are hard to clean. A great price on a simple model with a five-year warranty is the **Omega FoodPro Premier Food Processor O660**, for sale on multiple websites. • Ultimate Nourishment's website now offers a blender mixer combination that may be a good alternative, made by Blendtec.
Grass-fed butter	• A local, natural-food store • A local farm with a cow-share program (contact your local chapter of the Weston A. Price Foundation to find a farm near you) • The Organic Valley website (click on "Where to Buy" and check the box for grass-fed butter to see the closest market near you that sells this product) • Online sources (including Organic Pastures if you live in California)
Grass-fed gelatin	• Great Lakes brand or Vital Proteins • Amazon.com
Juicer	• Craigslist (for a used one) • A local kitchen store • Online from Ultimate Nourishment
Organic grass-fed ghee	• A local, natural-food store • Online at Amazon.com
Organic herbs, teas and vanilla	• Local farms and farmer's markets • Online at Mountain Rose Herbs

Organic nuts and seeds	• A local farm or farmer's market • A local, natural-food store (if it has excellent turnover on nuts and seeds) • Online from Hummingbird Wholesale (Located in Eugene, Oregon, this retailer offers the freshest nuts I've found, protecting consumers from the risks of rancidity. Sprout or freeze your nuts right when you receive them.)
Organic produce	• A local farmer's market • A local, natural-food store
Pasture-raised meat	• A local farm or farmer's market (see Eatwild.com to find a farm near you) • A local gourmet meat market — sometimes they carry grass-fed meat • A local natural-food store • Online at U.S. Wellness Meats
Raw milk	• A local dairy or farm with a cow-share program (see your local chapter of the Weston A. Price Foundation to find farms in your area) • Many natural-food markets carry local, raw goat's milk. • Varies state to state and country to country
Stevia	• A local natural-food store • Online at NuNaturals (free shipping and lots of other fun products, like stevia-sweetened chocolate syrup) • Online at Mountain Rose Herbs (you can order pure green leaf stevia powder or cut leaf stevia) • Your own garden (growing and steeping fresh stevia yields a milder flavor and is rewarding in its own right; special thanks to Maria Loftin for this idea!)
Water filter	• A local kitchen store (BPA-free pitchers are available) • Online at Amazon.com (which also carries BPA-free pitchers) and Radiant Life.com (which offers a super-safe stainless-steel option) • Berkey brand is highly recommended.

APPENDIX 2

Methods

How to Soak Beans

Like grains, nuts and most seeds, legumes need to be soaked to reduce phytates and enzyme inhibitors. When foods go through this process we consider them "predigested." Their nutrients are now easily accessed and utilized, as well as being gentle on our bodies' digestive mechanisms. Here's how: For every 2 cups beans, add 2 tablespoons apple cider vinegar or lemon juice, plus enough simmering water to cover. Let beans soak for 12 to 24 hours. (Kidney-shaped beans are the exception: They should be soaked with a pinch of baking soda for 12 to 24 hours with simmering water poured over — no acid medium.) Try to change out the acid or base water solution, refreshing with new water and either the acid or baking soda, two to three times during the soaking period for maximum digestibility. After the soaking period, rinse the beans well and then cook for 4 to 8 hours, until tender.

How to Soak and Sprout Nuts, Seeds and Peanuts

Soaking and Sprouting Nuts

Equipment needed: a dehydrator (or see options below)

For every 4 cups raw seeds or nuts, cover by two inches with room-temperature filtered water and 2 teaspoons sea salt. Stir well to dissolve the salt. Leave uncovered at room temperature overnight, then drain and rinse well in the morning. They are now ready to be used in their wet form for many of my recipes (or dehydrated in a dehydrator for 24 to 72 hours, depending on the kind of nut; after dehydration, sprouted nuts are often referred to as "crispy nuts"). If you are not ready to use the nuts or dehydrate them, once they have been rinsed, they keep well for a full week loosely covered in the refrigerator.

Dehydrating can be done at temperatures ranging from 95 to 145 degrees Fahrenheit. Some ovens or bread warmers will maintain this temperature well. So purchasing a dehydrator might not be necessary if you do not already own one.

Note: If you suspect that rancidity could be an issue with your nuts, which is common with cashews or any nuts that do not have a fast turnover on store shelves, add up to an 1/8 teaspoon grapefruit seed extract or vitamin C powder to your soaking water, stirring well to dissolve. This will kill any potential mold.

How to Make Homemade Almond (or Other Nut) Butter

Place 3 to 6 cups sprouted nut of choice (base the quantity of nuts on the size of your food processor) into work bowl of food processor. Process nuts for several minutes until they are liquified. In some cases, almonds will stay powdery. There are two solutions for this: Roast almonds in a 350-degree-Fahrenheit oven for approximately 20 minutes to release their oils, stirring one time at the halfway point. You may also add 1 to 2 tablespoons fat of choice: coconut oil, animal fat or my new favorite, cocoa butter! Season finished nut butter with sea salt, to taste.

How to Make Chia Seed Meal

Place 2 cups chia seeds into a high-powered blender and process for 10 seconds on medium-high speed.

How to Cook a Kabocha Squash

Preheat oven to 375 degrees Fahrenheit.

1. Using a long, sharp knife, poke a hole into the seed cavity of the squash, which will allow steam to escape.
2. Bake squash for 1-1/2 hours, placed on a cookie sheet to catch drips, or until very tender when poked deeply with a knife.

3. Allow it to cool slightly and then cut it in half height-wise, through the middle, as if cutting a "hat" off.

4. Open the lid of the squash and scoop the seeds from the seed cavity.

5. Measure out the recipe's designated amount of winter squash.

Alternative High-Heat Fats

When cooking items that utilize high heat, such as waffles, the best fat choices are ghee, avocado oil or animal fat. Coconut oil is also useful for medium-high temperatures. For this reason, I like the convenience of using coconut oil spray when making waffles. However, this may not be an ideal choice for everyone, because there are usually one or two non-whole food ingredients in coconut oil spray. If you prefer not to use it, try one of the high-heat fats. These can be applied with a heat-proof brush, or the fat can be frozen or chilled into a block and rubbed onto the iron.

APPENDIX 3

AIP Recipes

Carrot Flour | 14
Granny Smith Applesauce | 16
Coconut Syrup | 24
AIP Pancakes | 25

The following pies have nut crusts in this book. However, one of the bonus videos offers a lovely AIP crust. Sign up here for the free videos: www.eatbeautiful.net/free-videos

Pumpkin Pie Bar Filling | 81
Kiwi Lime Pie Filling | 92
Mixed Berry-Avocado Pie Filling | 94
Pumpkin Pie Filling | 99
Blackberry (or Apple) Pie Filling | 106

Marshmallow Root and Slippery Elm Porridge for One, seed-free variation | 143
Winter Squash Porridge | 147
Shepherd's Pie | 170
Coconut Whipped Cream | 184
Vanilla Date Shake "Ice Cream" | 193
Carrot Cinnamon Frozen Yogurt | 197
Cranberry-Mixed Berry Compote | 199
Pumpkin Butter with Strawberries | 208
Homemade Coconut Milk | 214
Stevia Lemonade | 220
Tarragon or Basil Limeade with Honey | 221

"Juiced Tea" — Marionberry Rooibos with Honey | 222
Cilantro-Mint Lassi variation (dairy-free) | 225
Ginger-Honey Milkshake | 227
Marionberry Panna Cotta variation (dairy-free) | 232
Colorful Gelatin | 235–236
Pumpkin Spice Pudding variation (dairy-free) | 238
Dairy-Free Parfaits | 247
Egg-Free and/or Dairy-Free Parfaits | 248

Made in the USA
San Bernardino, CA
23 July 2015